Worship and Politics

Worship and Politics

RAFAEL AVILA

*Translated from the Spanish
by Alan Neely*

ORBIS BOOKS
Maryknoll, New York 10545

The Catholic Foreign Mission Society of America (Maryknoll) recruits and trains people for overseas missionary service. Through Orbis Books Maryknoll aims to foster the international dialogue that is essential to mission. The books published, however, reflect the opinions of their authors and are not meant to represent the official position of the society.

First published as *Apuntes sobre las implicaciones socio-políticas de la Eucaristía* by Policrom Artes Gráficas, Bogotá, Colombia, copyright © 1977 by Rafael Avila P.

English translation copyright © 1981 by Orbis Books, Maryknoll, NY 10545

Manufactured in the United States of America

Manuscript Editor: William E. Jerman

Library of Congress Cataloging in Publication Data

Avila P., Rafael.
  Worship and politics.

  Translation of: Apuntes sobre las implicaciones socio-políticas de la Eucaristía.
  Includes bibliographical references and index.
  1. Lord's Supper—Catholic Church. 2. Catholic Church—Liturgy. 3. Sociology, Christian (Catholic) 4. Fasts and feasts—Judaism—History. 5. Liberation theology. I. Title.
BX2215.2.A9313   264'.02036   81-38356
ISBN 0-83844-714-2 (pbk.)   AACR2

"Zeal for the promotion and restoration of the liturgy is rightly held to be a sign of the providential dispositions of God in our time, as a movement of the Holy Spirit in his church."

—Vatican II, Constitution
on the Sacred Liturgy, No. 43

"For the liturgy is made up of *unchangeable elements* divinely instituted, and *elements subject to change*. The latter not only may but ought to be changed. . . ."

—Vatican II, ibid., No. 21

Contents

Translator's Foreword

The center of the church's life is . . . is what? When I raised this question recently with some of my colleagues, there was a dissonant chorus of responses. The center of the church's life—according to the more theologically inclined—is Jesus Christ. Others insisted that it is the worship of God. The functionally oriented chimed in with opinions covering the whole gamut of Christian involvement. It is evangelism, they said, *plantatio ecclesiae,* catechesis, fellowship *(koinonia),* spiritual formation and renewal. No less vigorous were those who asserted that the center of the church's life is (or should be) the penetration and transformation of society's macrostructures, the promotion of human welfare, liberation, and *diaconia.* Amid this concert—or was it a cacophony—of thinkers and doers I wondered if any single thought or act could encompass adequately the nucleus of the life of God's people.

The ecumenical conference on World Mission and Evangelism meeting in Melbourne, Australia, in May 1980 declared: "The centre of the Church's life is the Eucharist, the public declaration of thanksgiving for God's gift in Christ, and the participation in the very life of Christ."

Many would doubtless agree that the Eucharist *should be* the focal point of the Church's life, but as the reader of this provocative work will discover, Rafael Avila regards the current Eucharistic observance more as a source of alienation than a means of communion, more a sanctioning of the status quo than a stimulus to reform, more a residual cultism than a commitment or recommitment of believers to the precept and praxis of loving one's neighbor.

The significance of Avila's essay is not, however, his critique of contemporary theology and practice, but rather his proposed design of a Eucharist for the future. He refers to it as "design of a Eucharist for Latin America," but the implications of what he outlines reach far beyond the geographical, cultural, or sectarian limits of that continent.

When I was asked to translate Avila's book, I began frankly with a conditioned aloofness to the theme and expected that Avila's treatment would be far removed from the experiences of my own Protestant Free Church tradition. I was in for a jarring and transforming experience. I found that it called into question several unfounded assumptions. It uncovered subliminal biases. It revealed a shameful ignorance of my own knowledge of Judeo-Christian history. It pushed me to the limits of rethinking what has become in the life of my church not the "participation of the disciples in the very life of Christ," but a dull, unimaginative repetition of ecclesiastical ritual.

I had to answer the question for myself at least; if the Eucharist is the center of the church's life, why have some of us trivialized it by "tacking it on" to the end of the corporate worship experience? If the Eucharist is the center of the church's life, why have some of my Christian brothers and sisters so supernaturalized it with an aura of sorcery accompanied by incantations and smells far removed from the sweat, tears, pain, thirst, and death of the Carpenter of Nazareth? If the Eucharist is the center of the church's life, why have all of us so spiritualized, depoliticized, and a-historicized the broken bread and poured-out wine so that no one remembers or is reminded of the fact that Jesus' death (as is the death of millions today) was the result of a religio-political coalition of those who wanted to protect and perpetuate their social and economic positions? The center of the church's life can be, however, the collective remembering of what those words mean, "This is my body. . . this is my blood . . . broken . . . shed for you."

I first met Rafael Avila shortly after he had been dismissed from his teaching position in the Jesuit university of Bogotá—the result of growing opposition to the use of his seminal text, *La liberación,* written for high school religious study in Colombia and first published in 1969. Ironically, the book was so well received that a second edition was issued in 1971 but soon raised the ire of powerful groups who regarded it as subversive.

In contrast to some persons I have known, Rafael was not embittered nor intimidated by his experience. He continued to write, to teach, and to struggle for the total liberation of the *pueblo.* This work, *Worship and Politics,* was his fifth book published in Spanish and now his first in English. Avila is not a clergyman, nor has he ever sensed this kind of calling. His formal study of theology both in Colombia and in Europe came as a result of an inquisitive mind and commitment to people, especially to the poor and the oppressed. His theological perspective is not inhibited by an adherence to out-dated traditions. Yet he is not a reckless iconoclast. He knows the past and has gleaned the best from it. His comprehensive accounting and interpretation of the meaning of Christian history, and his proposal for a new history will, I believe, stimulate all of us to rethink and recast this, the central *sacramentum.*

ALAN NEELY

Preface to the English Translation

I have thought it best to provide a special preface to the English translation of this work. I wish first to point out that the reflections that follow are made in the context of the specific situation of Latin America, and more specifically still in that of Colombia, where they originated, although the scope of the problems they treat certainly goes beyond the limits of that country and raises more general questions.

I wish next to point out that the text has been translated with little change of content from the original Spanish version published in 1977.

Thirdly, I wish to enlarge a little, for the benefit of English-speaking readers, on the historical experience that stimulated these reflections and the sort of questions that they raised in my mind. I want to lay particular stress on this last point.

These notes were written under the impact of the general critique of religion addressed by Camilo Torres to the Christian world, not so much by his words as by his actions and finally by his death. The Camilo phenomenon was a sign of contradiction for Christians and non-Christians, a stumbling block that divided Christians down the middle. Camilo, after his fashion, conceived the church and its pastoral and liturgical activity as being of one piece with the dominant culture; he perceived with great perspicacity that its overall social function produced a system of injustices, later to be labeled by Medellín "institutionalized violence" and judged theologically to be a situation of sin.

Later some priests tried to work the struggle of the people into the Eucharist. This required improvisation, imagination, and risks. Many priests were scandalized by it, because things so "worldly" and "secular" as the struggle of the people were now being brought within the so-called specifically religious ambit, and this meant a dangerous infiltration of the prophetic spirit into precincts hitherto jealously monopolized by priestly castes.

The author of this work, for his part, took the option of considering those attempts as *indications* of a divorce between the socio-political reality and the liturgy, and, consequently, as insights and sketches of what needs to be reworked critically with the aid of a theoretical framework. What is presupposed here is that there exists a link between the material basis of human existence and the development of culture—not a direct mechanical link, but an indirect one, in the sense that the religious factor is not unique, not isolated, even though it retains a certain relative autonomy.

The modernizing winds of Vatican II introduced, nevertheless, one belated variation with regard to another current of Christian thinking, a variation that we may call "cultural adaptation" or "folklorization." This, not without difficulties, has been introduced progressively in Latin America. With it several things have been introduced into the liturgy: folk customs and clothes, native musical instruments, and even the dance, in which the body celebrates rhythmically its unlimited possibilities of expression, rebelling against the confinement of the human spirit within any rigid liturgical, socio-cultural, or socio-political mold. It was the beginning of reconciliation between liturgy and culture. Liturgy began to recover its festive character, rejecting all excessive formalism.

This change is undoubtedly necessary, and in my opinion there is still much to do in this area. But I should like to go further. A liturgy limited merely to reflecting the prevailing culture runs the risk of masking the type of social relationships underlying the culture, and so it would mask also the institutionalized violence and the sin of the world, thus reinforcing the dominant culture and the drive to control by dominant classes.

Hence the main aim in this work has been to show that the liturgy is inseparable not only from the specific culture of each people, but even and especially from the social relations of production proper to each social formation, and from the history thereof.

It is necessary to show, behind the activity of cultural reappropriation, the wider socio-political context and the connection between means of production, socio-economic relationships, and the production of culture, one of whose multiple expressions is the liturgy.

I not only feel that this is necessary, but I feel a responsibility to point out how politically dangerous it is to attempt a reappropriation of culture in isolation from the overall political interests of the masses of the people. Such an attempt would mislead us into clothing in national respectability what is really a drive to domination, when what we need is precisely to expose it to view, taking the culture of the people as our point of departure.

One could go further. The dominant classes would have no difficulty in promoting projects of folklorization or cultural adaptation even in the liturgical field, because that would be for them a marvelous ideological tactic for giving them legitimacy through the powerful psycho-social medium of the liturgy, or at least for keeping the forces of popular aggression dammed up. That would be nothing less than to poison the people with a sugared pill, destroying their hope at its roots with a "folklorized" liturgy that has only the appearance of being national.

A church not aware of this danger could be unknowingly helping to inject into the people the ideology and the projects of the dominant culture, and consequently converting into a "popular" religion the ideology of the dominant class. This would be to turn the liturgy into a platform for proclaiming not the good news of liberation, but the bad news of alienation, disguised in the gilded sophistries of "cultural adaptation."

If with this work I succeed at least in calling attention to the *political risk* of such a tendency, I shall feel I have done something more than raising a lone voice in the wilderness.

Worship and Politics

Introduction

Many Christians are experiencing today a certain amount of discomfort and nonconformity in regard to the Eucharist. For some it means very little, for others nothing at all. Many believers wonder whether the Eucharist survives as a residue of superstition or as a ceremony of compliance and alienation. There are those also who could not care less whether they participate or do not participate.

I have known several couples over the past few years for whom either the husband or the wife has to "screw up courage" even to accompany the other to Mass. Some of them object to certain kinds of preaching they hear. They feel terribly alienated by the formalism that they say is not unlike that of passengers on a bus who sit side by side but at the same time feel a miserable aloneness. "Where is communion in all of this," they ask, "if we are not sharing the word, the bread, the wine, as well as the time together? Instead of communion, we feel like outsiders, spectators who can only observe the minister as he celebrates *his* Mass."

Are there exceptions? Yes, but one can hardly see in them any kind of encouraging pattern, because they are insignificant in comparison with the accepted traditional practice. A communion service in which there is authentic sharing does not have the support of the majority of the faithful, much less that of the hierarchy. Such services are considered to be deviations.

Can a believer look with indifference at this anomaly? By no means, and certainly not when one honestly believes oneself to have a theological responsibility. Theologians worthy of the name begin their work by reflecting on the real problems believers face. They feel challenged by these problems and want to help solve them; such is their charism. When the Eucharist fails to exert any significant influence in the life of the church, and when Christians feel estranged by the sacrament, something is seriously amiss. We feel compelled to attempt to determine the cause.

To assert that the results of Vatican Council II were not implemented, or that they were poorly applied, or, as some have recklessly charged, that it was a grievous error to allow the Mass to be said in the vernacular—a reform that Protestant Christians instituted four centuries ago—simply does not correspond to reality.

The very opposite is the case. Despite the resistance encountered (and resistance is experienced with any historical initiative), Vatican II instituted changes very slowly. Today—and this is the problem—everything possible has been done to attain its objectives even though they were very limited and did not go far enough.

Many would like to see the church function as a kind of "clandestine agency" and the gospel guarded jealously as a "state secret." Nothing, however, would be more at variance with the proclaimed policy of "opening the windows." The church has received a mandate to proclaim from the housetops what has been heard in private (Matt. 10:27) and to "expound things hidden since the foundation of the world" (Matt. 13:35).[1] Can it be that some fear the possibilities that would accompany a truly heraldic Eucharist?

We know that the apocalyptic inquisitor will hasten to announce the decline of faith in Latin America, that witch hunters will allege the infiltration of communism, that the pious but ingenuous hierarchy will lament the abandoning of customs among the people, that there will be those who express a "basic lack of confidence in prayer," and that all these anomalies will be attributed to the imprudences of certain priests.

What really is taking place in Latin America? This question is the primary and simple preoccupation of this small work. Without attempting to give a complete response, we will look at certain causes (elements for diagnosis) and will conclude by proposing certain components for the designing of a Eucharist for Latin America (steps for solution) and analogous contexts.

Those who minimize the role of the religious superstructure on our continent and its function in shaping the popular Latin

American mind will be surprised by this "cultual anxiety" of the author.

The truth is that the so-called subjective conditions—that is, the ideology of the people—are really objective conditions, "effective and concrete obstacles that trip up or ensnare revolutionaries."[2]

The Eucharist, on the other hand, although celebrating the most radical of liberations, has been so extravagantly barricaded with rubrical "sandbags" that, rather than being a bridge between the sign and the people, it has become in reality a wall that must be demolished. This can be accomplished, however, only with great difficulty by well-trained elites and sufficiently patient individuals who have not given up. That the Eucharist proclaim what it celebrates in a comprehensive language of words and signs and that it completely cease being a mysterious logomachy is what we desire and nothing more. That it therefore represent the word and not the silence of the people, the word clearly articulated and not mumbled or stammered, that it celebrate the liberation and not the hidden enslavement of the people, is what we desire.

With this perspective in mind we will first of all examine the origins of the Judeo-Christian tradition in order to recover for the present the heritage of hope that this tradition inspires. No one should doubt our fidelity to the past; this fidelity, however, does not consist in conserving or merely repeating the past, but rather unlocking and releasing it. For only human beings have the ability to review the past and to correct the mistakes of the present.

The conservative mania to preserve the past—as if this were preservation—impedes the vital impulses of the past and fossilizes it, thus provoking an abortion of a gestation that was begun with great difficulty. The mania to preserve the past also manifests a kind of necrophilia, because to bring gestation to a standstill is to abort it.

In this work we shall examine the past, attempting to be faithful to the struggles of our ancestors and to their noblest intuitions, believing that these efforts have not been in vain and that they open anew avenues that have been closed. In other words, we shall return to the past in order to renew our hope. Our search, in the last analysis, should open a way for us to move toward the goal.

Those who close off the past are unfaithful to it and are the accomplices of those who "stifled" the prophets. The blood of the prophets cries out against them.

We are aware that our perspective restricts us to a certain selectivity because we do not return to the past in pursuit of relics, but rather in search of landmarks that can assist us in achieving our basic purpose. We return to the past not motivated by *it,* but rather motivated by the present. The anthropologist, for example, does not have the same interest in fossils as does a rockhound. Rather the anthropologist is interested in fossils in order to reconstruct the evolutionary stages in prehistory. The historian—and theology is a historical science—functions in the same way. Historians return to the past in order to discover the etiology of the present.

This selectivity is one of the indispensable elements in the reinterpretation of history. And inasmuch as the Eucharist is a composite expression of history (reflecting its total language of words and signs), it is susceptible to a reinterpretation from the perspective of the Latin American prophetic conscience. This would logically presuppose considerable spadework to understand the reinterpretation of the entire Judeo-Christian tradition,[3] the Eucharist being a particular example within that reinterpretation. The urgency of the situation in Latin America, however, obliges us to attempt this reinterpretation without having developed or perfected its characterization.

If we look to the past it is in order to be certain of our continuity with the Judeo-Christian tradition. But to limit ourselves to that one certainty—namely, our continuity with the Judeo-Christian tradition—would be irresponsible. We are not merely preservers of the past. We are principally recreative agents of living tradition. For this reason we believe ourselves obliged to risk a discontinuity with the past by proposing a new Eucharist, and in this sense we understand our effort as a faithfulness to and an expression of responsibility toward our tradition.

It should be noted, on the other hand, that this tradition has considered the Eucharist as a referential sacrament. What is said of the Eucharist will, *mutatis mutandis,* raise questions about other sacramental expressions, and in turn about the entire liturgy.

CHAPTER ONE

The Passage from the Mesopotamian and Canaanite Rites to the Rite of Israel (Reinterpretation I)

Following the exodus, Israel acquired a distinctive historical consciousness together with a new set of rites. These rites became the cultic objectification of history and historico-political reactivators.

The religion and cult of Israel passed through various stages before they finally crystalized. We will attempt here to outline these developments in summary fashion.

When Joshua assembled the tribes at Shechem, he reminded them of their common past by declaring:

Yahweh, the God of Israel, says this: "In ancient days your ancestors lived beyond the River—such as Terah the father of Abraham and of Nahor—and they served other gods" [Josh. 24:2].

The river to which Joshua alluded was surely the Euphrates, and beyond the Euphrates were situated the Mesopotamian and Chaldean cultures. The reference of course is to the ancestors of Abraham who belonged to those Mesopotamian and Chaldean cultures, and who doubtless were devotees of the religion predominant in that area of the world. Professor John Bright contends that Ur and Haran were both "centers of the moon cult."[1] The predominant religions during this period were cosmological, animistic, and fertility cults, all with multiple myths of origins.

The Break with the Chaldean Religion

The second phase of development in the Jewish religion may be characterized as that of the break or separation from the Chaldean religion. The biblical tradition records the data reflective of that historic transition.

The first of these is the migration (?) of Terah, the father of Abraham, from Ur of the Chaldees to Haran in Mesopotamia:

> Terah took his son Abram, his grandson Lot the son of Haran, and his daughter-in-law the wife of Abram, and made them leave Ur of the Chaldeans to go to the land of Canaan. But on arrival in Haran they settled there [Gen. 11:31].

I have placed a question mark after the word "migration" because another passage would seem to call for a different interpretation. Note the following from the book of Judith:

> These people are descended from the Chaldeans. They once came to live in Mesopotamia, because they did not want to follow the gods of their ancestors who lived in Chaldea. They abandoned the way of their ancestors to worship the God of heaven, the God they had learned to acknowledge. *Banished* from the presence of their own gods, they fled to Mesopotamia where *they lived* for a long time [Jth. 5:6-8].[2]

When one reads in the first text that Abram, Sarah, and Lot left "Ur of the Chaldeans to go to the land of Canaan," but settled first in "Haran" in Mesopotamia, it is logical to conclude that this was a group of nomad adventurers who were tranquilly seeking another place of residence for no particular reason other than their own personal initiative. But upon examining the passage in Judith it becomes evident that they were exiles and that their leaving Ur was not by personal choice or a decision made without cause. Rather they were expelled from Ur for socio-religious reasons. Thus we are dealing with a conflict not simply religious, but a conflict fraught with social and political overtones. And they had been banished or expelled, it is obvious, "because they did not want to follow the gods of their ancestors." The conflict resulted from the fact that Abram and the others had "abandoned the way of their ancestors to worship the God of heaven." The root of the historic break, therefore, was a religious experience of sufficient magnitude to prompt Abram and the others to deny the gods of their fathers.

The second phase in this development may be seen in the departure of Abram from Haran to Canaan (Gen. 12:1–5). Terah dies, and Abram faces the difficult choice of returning to his own land—Chaldea—or of consolidating the break by separating completely his clan from the Chaldean culture and religion. He was deciding therefore not only his future but also that of his descendants, who would suffer the consequences of his decision. Apparently what Abram had vaguely perceived—upon continuing his pilgrimage—became clearer, for the texts indicate that his setting forth for the land of Canaan was inspired by the concept of the project of fashioning a new people (Gen. 12:2).

The real emphasis in these passages is not so much that of the *ex-odus* ("leave your country"), but rather the *eis-odus* ("for the land I will show you"). In the experience of leaving, "Abraham went as Yahweh told him . . . they set off." The God that Abram and his family had recognized is experienced as the one who commanded them to set forth ("Leave your country, your family, and your father's house"). And the land to which they moved is perceived as that indicated by God ("for the land I will show you"). The nation that God promised to fashion, a nation without relationship with the parent tribe, is perceived as a people that God would make by means of Abram himself ("I will make you a great nation"). And the conquest that they were obliged to initiate, and which his descendants would culminate, is experienced as the conquest of the land that God would give to Abram and his family ("It is to your descendants that I will give this land," Gen. 12:7).

Utilization of the Canaanite Holy Places

Abram Constructs Altars to Yahweh

Abram passed through the land as far as Shechem's holy place, the oak of Moreh. At that time the Canaanites were in the land. Yahweh appeared to Abram and said, "It is to your descendants that I will give this land." So Abram built there an altar for Yahweh, who had appeared to him [Gen. 12:6–8].

The "holy place" was already there before the arrival of Abram. It was a place set aside by the Canaanites for worship. The incidental clause, "at that time the Canaanites were in the land," is a clear indication of the nature of those places of worship. The particular spot was associated with a tree, for the Mesopotamian as well as the Canaanite religions considered certain places sacred, such as Ophra, Jerusalem, Gerizim; certain waters or wells such as Kadesh, Gihon, and the well of Jacob; various trees such as the terebinth and the oak of Tabor, the palm of Deborah, and the oak of Mamre; and certain high places such as Mounts Hermon, Tabor, Carmel, Sinai, and Zion.[3]

Abram utilized this place of worship, but he built on it an altar to Yahweh. At first glance it would appear that Abram had merely followed the custom of his Canaanite neighbors in the use of this holy place. But the fact is that in setting aside the place for the worship of Yahweh (Jth. 5:8) Abram's worship was intrinsically and profoundly distinct, for the altar was not built to the Canaanite gods but rather to Yahweh. Here is the beginning of some momentous ramifications which initially are impossible to differentiate, but with the passing of time their nature becomes evident.

The construction of altars by Abram and his descendants followed the norms of the times: Moses built an altar at the foot of Mount Sinai and erected twelve stones for the twelve tribes of Israel (Exod. 24:4). Joshua took a great stone and set it up at

Shechem as a testimony of the commitment of the tribes (Josh. 24:26). From the beginning the leaders of Israel were well aware that they were using the Canaanite places of worship, but Israel had its own God, and it was this God who was directing their worship. Jacob, for example, erected an altar at Shechem and he invoked "El, God of Israel" (Gen. 33:20).

This phase in the history of Israel was of course characterized by a certain degree of syncretism. The Israelites took pride in the fact that at the beginning their God *also* had an altar as did other gods, and they moved from this initial stage in which they were conforming to the environment and in which their God coexisted peacefully with the Canaanite deities. Yahweh had an altar alongside the altars of Baal and Asherah. This is the stage of *also our God.* They recognized their God as different, but they were not yet aware of the fact that their God was a jealous God. The experience of the exodus would be necessary before they would recognize this distinction.

The Sanctuaries as Depositories of History

There is still another aspect that will awaken us to the peculiarity of the Israelite cult. The altars they constructed in the Canaanite holy places "mark the route of the patriarchs."[4]

It should be remembered that Shechem was the first stop of Abram (Gen. 12:6). When Jacob returned from Mesopotamia he also camped there and erected a new altar to "El, God of Israel" (Gen. 33:18–20). Joshua convened the twelve tribes of Israel there (Josh. 24:25). Doubtless the evangelist had these historical events in his mind when he wrote: "Jesus, tired by the journey, sat straight down by the well" (John 4:6).

Jacob sensed that God could not coexist with idols and therefore said to his clan and those who accompanied them, "Get rid of the foreign gods you have with you" (Gen. 35:2). Joshua also said—although this was already postexodus—to the tribes that had come together for their unification: "Cast away the alien gods among you and give your hearts to Yahweh, the God of Israel" (Josh. 24:23). We should also remember that Joshua was buried at Shechem.

At Bethel, in his second encampment in Canaan, Abraham

erected a new altar (Gen. 12:8; 13:4). And Jacob had his dream of the ladder standing on the ground with its top reaching to heaven, and here he took the stone that he had used for his pillow and set it up as an altar, pouring oil over the top of it and naming it Bethel (Gen. 28:10–22). Subsequently at this same place Jacob's descendants would congregate to offer sacrifices, substituting the cult of a Canaanite deity for that of Yahweh.

At Mamre Abraham erected another altar, and there in a cave he, together with other patriarchs and their wives, was buried (Gen. 23:1–20). Also it was here at Mamre (Hebron) that Abraham had some of his most profound religious experiences. Thus the place was identified with the development of the Hebrew faith. "One may say that the worship expressed the significant and perennial content of the history of the patriarchs, of their pilgrimages, of their religious experiences, and of their expressions of faith."[5]

As the Israelites returned from time to time to those sacred places they were able to retrace the thread of the history of their ancestors.

They believed that their God was the same God of their fathers, and that they were one with their ancestors: "My father was a wandering Aramaean. He went down into Egypt to find refuge there" (Deut. 26:5). To return to those places was like rereading the heroic deeds of the patriarchs in such a way as to reassume their historical past by submitting themselves progressively to the awareness of the unity of their history and of their God. The unity of the people among themselves and with their god was indivisible. In the way in which they were characterized as a people, they also characterized their God and their worship.

Conclusion

In these sanctuaries or holy places—all of which were Canaanite—the religious experience of Israel had special characteristics.

In the first place, the patriarchs singled out their own God for worship, but they made provision for the Canaanite divinities also. After returning from Egypt, however, as we will see, these Canaanite gods were removed.

Secondly, as a consequence, worship had a different meaning

for the patriarchs, even though, according to cultural standards, they were not very distinct from the Canaanite forms.

Finally, myths of the beginnings (Mesopotamian) and the myths of nature (Canaanite) allowed for the accumulation of historical data that became a part of the collective memory of the people.

The Experience of the Exodus

The Incorporation of History into Religious Rites

Without question the exodus from Egyptian slavery constituted the principal event in the development of Israel's public worship as a people.

The liberation from Egyptian slavery (the exodus) was for the Israelites an event similar to the Battle of Boyacá for us Colombians. It marked the transition from being a colony of slaves to that of an independent nation. The history of Israel actually begins with the exodus when the clans or family groups united under the leadership of Moses to march toward their freedom. Thus God formed a people or nation, and the covenant between them was finally sealed at Sinai.

With this pact Yahweh became the God of Israel, and Israel became the people of God (Lev. 26:12). And in gratitude for their freedom, the Israelites consecrated themselves to Yahweh and gave themselves to him as a bride surrenders herself to the embrace of her husband.

It was a kind of *matrimonial commitment,* as the prophet Ezekiel describes it in his allegorical history (16:9-10). For this reason when Israel subsequently abandoned Yahweh for other gods, the prophets labeled their behavior infidelity and adultery (Hos. 2:5; 3:1-3). It was natural, therefore, that Israel should celebrate its independence with a festival, and this religious festival was the passover.

The passover was, however, a pastoral and an agricultural celebration of springtime that commemorated "the liberation of the vital forces and the bursting out of new life that broke the grip of winter."[6] It celebrated the resurrection of nature from winter's death.

When the Hebrews began to enjoy their freedom—that is, after leaving Egypt—*the passover assumed a new meaning for them.* It commemorated not only the emergence of new life from the dormant period of winter, but also the liberation from Egyptian slavery. *Thus the liberation of nature's vital forces began to be associated with the historical liberation,* and spring would become the time for celebrating the liberating intervention of God in their history. The passover would therefore commemorate God's emancipating act.

What God had done for his people in freeing them from Egyptian servitude, he continued doing in the ritual celebration of the passover, liberating from their enslavement those who participated in this act of worship.[7]

A springtime setting for the passover celebration memorialized liberation of life, and the varied ritualistic elements of the celebration brought to mind the exodus from Egypt, thereby impregnating Israel with the idea of liberating and forging in their collective consciousness a deeply ingrained desire for freedom and a profound aversion to any kind of enslavement.

The passover, therefore, celebrated the freedom of the people of God. Readings from their Scriptures and the teachings of the prophets constantly reminded the community of God's great intervention to liberate Israel, and their corporate experience served as a kind of laboratory in which the Israelites learned and relearned the history of their nation (commemoration). Israel gave thanks for these interventions that Yahweh had performed in their behalf, especially in view of the fact that they had been such an insignificant people (Deut. 7:6–8) but had been chosen and had been consecrated as "God's own people."

The passover was also a goal or stimulus for the nation. Israel periodically renewed the *commitment* which it had made at Sinai with the Liberator, and the people were reminded that the covenant involved an awesome responsibility. Yahweh, having chosen them, laid upon them a difficult mission: to be "the light of the nations so that my salvation may reach to the ends of the earth" (Isa. 49:6)—that is, to be the agent of God's project of liberation.

Israel recognized that the liberating activity of God continued in the passover celebration: that the movement toward freedom was already in motion and for this reason was projected toward a messianic future in which liberation would be more extraordinary than the exodus from Egypt and the covenant would be more demanding than that of Sinai.

In this form the passover allowed for a partial vision of the glorious *destiny* of the nation that inspired them to fulfill their mission and to continue their pilgrimage.[8]

With the incorporation of the exodus into the passover ritual, Yahweh established the foundations for the eventual and complete triumph over the agricultural divinities of the Canaanites, and the history of the nation becomes a part of their religious ritual. This emancipation history is the history that henceforth will be celebrated, and the ritual will involve the remembering of the historical event(s). Theirs will be a mobile memory in contradistinction to the sanctuaries of the patriarchal era, which were fixed memorials or memories of a place. Space gave way to time, and there was awakened a consciousness of temporality. God would now be the one who had liberated the people from their servitude, the one who was there in the beginning of the nation and who had accompanied them in their history.

This distinctive consciousness of their historicity that Israel acquired, beginning with the exodus, marked *a qualitative leap in the history of the nations,* and it generated a corresponding ritualistic character radically new and different. What occurred, therefore, was *a qualitative passage in the history of religious rites.* For the first time human beings utilized a rite to objectify (place before them) their history. The rite became a historical remembrance (a memorial), and the exodus became the central event around which the Hebrews organized their entire perception of reality.[9] This perception of reality could not be explained without the cultual objectification of it, which in turn obliged them to return continually to reality as their primordial and referential experience that generated and regenerated their consciousness as a nation. Without this, neither their tenacious historical consciousness nor their discovery of history as history can be explained.

Cultic Preservation of the Political Character of the Exodus

The collective and symbolic language by and in which Israel expressed its new historical consciousness is a different kind of rite. In reality, as we have already indicated, it is more than "the incorporation of the exodus into the ritual of the passover." It is rather the creation of a new rite. And by "new rite" we are not talking about a refurbishing of the old cosmological rites or of the natural evolution of those rites. Israel was not interested in re-forming the traditional ritual. Their historical consciousness created a new necessity, a new historical dynamic that needed a new ritualistic expression. The cosmos had been replaced by the new awareness of the crucial importance of history. To be sure some cosmological remnants remain, but the historical has as-sumed the primary importance. It is seized and re-formed, and in so doing the socio-political character of the event is maintained. It is not, however, mystified.

Worship does not depoliticize the event. On the contrary, it enhances the political implications of the event. Cultual objectifi-cation does not act as a political muffler, but as a historical reac-tivator. If the event has been objectified and placed before Israel in the rite as a mobile remembrance, it is *because* (and not in spite of) the fact that the event forms an integral part of the nation and will continually have to be reconsidered, thoroughly examined, and discerned in order that the faith of Israel will be in a continual process of revitalization.

For this reason I am not in agreement with the "cultists" who attempt to minimize the political character of the exodus by insist-ing that the goal of the exodus was to celebrate a liturgical rite. They cite the following biblical text:

> "I shall be with you," was the answer, "and this is the sign by which you shall know that it is I who have sent you. After you have led the people out of Egypt, you are to offer wor-ship to God on this mountain" [Exod. 3:12].
>
> They will listen to your words, and with the elders of Israel you are to go to the king of Egypt and say to him, "Yahweh, the God of the Hebrews, has come to meet us. Give us leave, then, to make a three days' journey into the wilderness to offer sacrifice to Yahweh our God" [Exod. 3:18].

From these and other texts they have attempted to support the position that the finality of the exodus was the cult—that is, an act essentially religious and not political—in order to conclude that the exodus can be classified and measured by its religious and cultic end. It would appear that those who interpret the text thus are finally forced, in light of the cumulative evidence, to admit that there was an exodus, but as a species of necessary evil to which God—as the enemy of political involvement—is obligated, not to liberate the people from their political and social yoke, but to have a people who will worship God without the religious restrictions that the pharaoh imposed. For the "cultists," the political event of the exodus is not in the strictest sense the salvific event, but merely the precondition of the covenant. It is the covenant, they would say, that is the salvific event (salvific for the people in the cultic sense). On the other hand, if the "cultists" are forced by the evidence to recognize that the exodus was in itself a salvific act, they must consider that it was salvific *in spite of* the fact that it was political and not *because* it was political.

When one begins to read these texts without these cult presuppositions, one immediately discovers that the cult was celebrated in the context of a historical liberation and not the reverse. The passover was to be eaten with "a girdle around your waist, sandals on your feet, a staff in your hand. You shall eat it hastily" (Exod. 12:11) as one beginning a journey. From the earliest time the worship was to be associated with the exodus, and the characteristics of the worship experience received their meaning from the exodus. The pivotal event then is the exodus. If the covenant at Sinai constitutes a new milestone, it does so primarily because it represents a development that concretizes the commitment of the people to God, who had brought them out of Egypt.[10]

God had indicated to Moses that he was to say to the pharaoh, "This is what Yahweh, the God of Israel, has said, 'Let my people go, so that they may keep a feast in the wilderness in honor of me' " (Exod. 5:1). But God had previously said to Moses, "I have seen the miserable state of my people in Egypt. I have heard their appeal to be free of their slave drivers. Yes, I am well aware of their sufferings. I mean to deliver them out of the hands of the Egyptians and to bring them up out of the land to a land rich and broad, a land where milk and honey flow" (Exod. 3:7–8). And also, "I have resolved to bring you up out of Egypt where you are oppressed" (Exod. 3:17). First and foremost is the exodus; it is strategic.

To go into the wilderness in order to celebrate a religious feast was merely a diversionary tactic of the fundamental strategy— namely, to escape once and for all the oppression of Egyptian slavery. When, for example, the pharaoh wearies of the repeated problems and sufferings related to keeping the Israelites in bondage, he agrees to allow them the freedom to worship on the condition that they not leave the country. He summons Moses and Aaron and says to them, "Go and offer sacrifice to your God, but in this country!" (Exod. 8:25). Moses replied that a journey of three days into the wilderness was necessary because "we sacrifice to Yahweh our God animals which Egyptians count it sacrilege to slaughter. If we offer in front of them sacrifices that outrage them, they will stone us" (Exod. 8:26–27). Moses was aware of the interrelation between national sovereignty and the freedom of worship, and he declared the *radical incompatibility* between the historical design of the pharaoh and those of the people of Israel.

Freedom of worship without national sovereignty is absurd, and for this reason Moses refused to celebrate the faith of Israel in the context of oppression. If Moses had been a cultist he would have easily fallen into the trap of a quasi liberty of worship exercised by slaves. But he refused, and his refusal constitutes another scandal for the cultists.

The covenant and the law (juridico-religious regulations) were always preceded by an obligatory prologue: "Say this to the house of Jacob, declare this to the sons of Israel, 'You yourselves have seen what I did with the Egyptians, how I carried you on eagles' wings and brought you to myself' " (Exod. 19:3b–4). "I am Yahweh your God who brought you out of the land of Egypt, out of the house of slavery" (Exod. 20:2). This was a refrain that the prophets used with vehemence when they wanted to make a proposal to the people or when they wanted to reproach the people for their sin.

From the Conquest to the Exile

Yahweh as a War God

When Israel, now free from Egyptian bondage, began the conquest of Canaan, it nourished the impression that the God of Israel maintained the same aggressiveness as did God's people.

The time had already passed when the patriarchs would be satisfied with a remote corner of the land for their God, and Israel refused to allow their God to coexist peacefully with the Canaanite deities. The enemies of Israel were the enemies of Yahweh, and vice versa:

> If you listen carefully to his voice [the angel's] and do all that I say, I shall be enemy to your enemies, foe to your foes. My angel will go before you and lead you to where the Amorites are and the Hittites, the Perizzites, the Canaanites, the Hivites, the Jebusites; I shall exterminate these [Exod. 23:22–23].

Yahweh would destroy the pagan gods in the same battles in which the people overcame the kings and their armies. And if the Israelites are victorious over them, unquestionably it was a victory over their gods. Any attempt to establish détente with them would also be an attempt to establish détente with their gods and their values. Yahweh prohibited all such pacts. It was to be a war to the death. It was to be either Yahweh or the pagan deities. Moreover, to accept the worship of a pagan people was considered to be an acceptance, a wooing, of the social, political, and cultural values that they maintained and with which they were identified. Also for Israel to worship pagan gods was to renounce its own cultural identity and risk its very survival as a people:

> You must not bow down to their gods or worship them; you must not do as they do: You must destroy their gods utterly and smash their standing stones [Exod. 23:24].
> You must make no pact with them or with their gods. They must not live in your country or they will make you sin against me; you would come to worship their gods, and that would be a snare for you indeed [Exod. 23:32–33].

The religious fervor that appeared subsequently is very explicit in this respect:

> Take care you make no pact with the inhabitants of the land you are about to enter, or this will prove a pitfall at your very feet. You are to tear down their altars, smash

their standing stones, cut down their sacred poles.

You shall bow down to no other god, for Yahweh's name is the Jealous One; he is a jealous God. Make no pact with the inhabitants of the land or, when they prostitute themselves to their own gods in sacrifice to them, they may invite you and you may consent to eat from their victims; or else you may choose wives for your sons from among their daughters and these, prostituting themselves to their own gods, may induce your sons to do the same [Exod. 34:12–16].

It would be a mistake, however, to see this as a theological struggle, a crusade, or a holy war. Israel was not fighting for a holy land or for a place for its God. Israel was struggling for a necessary living space for the people as a nation. This is not a religious or cultural epic but a national epic, as Roland de Vaux makes very clear:

When the people took up arms they were called the people of Yahweh or the people of God (Judg. 5:13; 20:2), the troops of God (1 Sam. 17:26), or the armies of Yahweh (Exod. 12:41; cf. 7:4). . . . The wars of Israel were the wars of Yahweh (1 Sam. 18:17; 25:28), and the national epic was sung of in the "Book of the Wars of Yahweh" (Num. 21:14), a book no longer extant. Israel did not fight for its faith, but for its existence.[11]

Expressions such as "I will exterminate them," "I will destroy them," and "I will cut down their sacred poles" indicate the aggressiveness that should be utilized against the other peoples and, more specifically, against the altars and shrines of the Canaanites. Israel was entering the phase of *only our God* (which, however, did not signify that they believed their God to be the only god). In order to establish the supremacy of their God they would have to unseat the gods to whom territorial sovereignty was accorded.

The word *baal* itself means "possessor," "owner," or "inhabitant." The Baalim of Canaan were the proprietors of certain activities or more frequently of particular towns and places. They were *immobile* gods. A particular baal expected deference from people only so long as they were within its territorial jurisdiction. The Baalim were the gods of a sedentary, settled people who were resistant to and suspicious of any kind of change.[12]

One can easily see, therefore, why the leaders prohibited the presence of the pagan gods (their standing stones or sacred poles) in the land of Israel. "They must not live in your country or they will make you sin against me" (Exod. 23:33). The reason was that the Canaanite gods were considered to be the proprietors of the territory in which they resided. It was necessary to dislodge them, to eradicate them and expropriate the land that they claimed as theirs. To expropriate a people from their god, it was necessary to expropriate their land. With the conquest and the appropriation of the territory, there was also appropriated their entire cultural universe. Yahweh would say therefore: "All the land within sight I will give to you and your descendants forever" (Gen. 13:15).

This accomplishment could have been done only by a mobile God who was none other than the God of the exodus, a God who walked before his people and with them in the cloud, in the tent, and above all in the ark of the covenant. "The key characteristics of Yahweh, the Old Testament God, are linked to his mobility. He is the Lord of history and time. He is not spatially placed. It was because Yahweh, like the Jews, was a nomad that the period of settlement in Canaan sparked the titanic battle between Yahweh and the baal."[13]

Just as nomads cannot be restricted to one place, so their link with their ancestors cannot be spatial or cosmological but must rather be temporal and historical. The Jews were descendants of Abraham, Isaac, and Jacob no matter where they were. For this reason the Israelite affirmation, "Yahweh, the God of your fathers, the God of Abraham, the God of Isaac, and the God of Jacob" (Exod. 3:15) refers to a temporal and historical God, not to a spatial and cosmological deity:

The de-spatialization of the deity moves in tandem with the appearance of God as active in historical events.

The nomadic life of the Israelites provided the necessary

social setting for the emergence of a view of God that was startlingly at variance with those of Israel's neighbors. Yahweh was a God of history, not of nature. He disclosed himself in political and military events, including defeats.[14]

Inhuman Rites Proscribed

The conquest revealed not only a new aspect of God, but also a new aspect of humankind. The religious prostitution of the Canaanites was explicitly condemned: "There must be no sacred prostitute among the daughters of Israel, and no sacred prostitute among the sons of Israel" (Deut. 23:18). Likewise the inhuman custom of burning infants in sacrifice was proscribed. The Hebrew prophets substituted for human sacrifice the sacrifice of animals, a rite that originally assured the preservation of the firstborn (Exod. 13:11-16). The sacrifice of Isaac was divinely disrupted (Gen. 22:11-12), a test which terminated thus: "Then looking up, Abraham saw a ram caught by its horns in a bush. Abraham took the ram and offered it as a burnt offering *in place of his son"* (Gen. 22:13). And the redemption of the firstborn of Israel culminated the liberating activity of God in freeing the people from Egyptian bondage. The Israelites may have practiced the immolation of their firstborn sons in a primitive phase of their development, as neighboring peoples did, but Exodus 13:14 and 34:19-20 indicate that the firstborn sons were to be redeemed. Later the prophets, such as Jeremiah and Ezekiel, would condemn the custom, emphatically and without hesitation, affirming that such a practice had absolutely no relationship to the will of Yahweh (Isa. 57:5; Jer. 7:31; 19:4-5; 32:35; Ezek. 16:20; Ps. 106:37). This process culminated with the promulgation of a severe law by which the community was ordered to stone any man who sacrificed his child to idols:

Any son of Israel or any stranger living in Israel must die if he hands over any of his children to Molech. The people of the country must stone him, and I shall set my face against that man and outlaw him from his people; for in handing over his children to Molech he has defiled my sanctuary and profaned my holy name [Lev. 20:2-4].

Likewise the consultation of the spirits of the dead or appealing to magicians was unequivocally condemned (Lev. 20:6), and anyone practicing these abominations was to be stoned: "Any man or woman who is a necromancer or magician must be put to death by stoning; their blood shall be on their own head" (Lev. 20:27).

The Religious Feasts of Justice

A preoccupation with justice was not alien to the liturgy of Israel, for it constitutes one of the basic concerns. It is possible to cite for example the following passages.

a. The Sabbatical Year:

> For six years you may sow your land and gather its produce, but in the seventh year you must let it lie fallow and forego all produce from it. Those of your people who are poor may take food from it and let the wild animals feed on what you leave. You shall do the same with your vineyards and your olive groves [Exod. 23:10–11].

Likewise, in the same year the debts of all the Israelites were to be canceled in order that there not be any poor among the people (Deut. 15:1–4). Also slaves were to be freed:

> If your fellow Hebrew, man or woman, is sold to you, he can serve you for six years. In the seventh year you must set him free, and in setting him free you must not let him go empty-handed. You must make him a generous provision from your flock, your threshing-floor, your winepress; as Yahweh your God has blessed you, so you must give to him [Deut. 15:12–14].

The moral and religious basis for this requirement was explicitly stated: "Remember that you were slaves in the land of Egypt and that Yahweh your God redeemed you; that is why I lay this charge on you today" (Deut. 15:15). Because Yahweh had liberated them, they were under divine mandate to liberate the enslaved among them.

b. The Feasts of Weeks and of Tabernacles: Other feasts were analogous to those of the sabbatical year, but they were to be celebrated with greater frequency. The conditions set forth for the observance of the Feast of Weeks are recorded in Deuteronomy 16:9–12, and for the Feast of Tabernacles in Deuteronomy 16:13–14. The purpose was to serve as a reminder to the Israelites "that you were a slave in Egypt" (16:12).

c. The Year of Jubilee: As has already been noted, the gods in the Canaanite cultural context were the proprietors or masters of the land areas with which they were associated. This association had not only religious but also social significance. The same came to be true for Israel, as the Mosaic law clearly states: "Land must not be sold in perpetuity, for the land belongs to me, and to me you are only strangers and guests," declared Yahweh (Lev. 25:23). The Jubilee Year (i.e., the fiftieth year), therefore, served the function of returning the land to the original owners:

> You will declare this fiftieth year sacred and proclaim the liberation of all the inhabitants of the land. This is to be a jubilee for you; each of you will return to his ancestral home, each to his own clan [Lev. 25:10].

The land was never considered to be the personal or private property of anyone, but was declared to be rather the property of Yahweh and his people in common. *The only thing that could be sold was the usufruct of the land, never the land itself,* as can be unquestionably inferred from the following text:

> If you buy from your neighbor, this must take into account the number of years since the jubilee: according to the number of productive years he will fix the price. The greater the number of years, the higher shall be the price demanded; the less the number of years, the greater the reduction; *for what he is selling you is a certain number of harvests* [Lev. 25:14–16].

This particular law guaranteed equity in real estate transactions and militated against the monopolizing of the land, a practice subsequently denounced by the prophets Isaiah and Micah:

Woe to those who add house to house
and join field to field
until everywhere belongs to them
and they are the sole inhabitants of the land [Isa. 5:8].

Woe to those who plot evil,
who lie in bed planning mischief!
No sooner is it dawn than they do it
—their hands have the strength for it.
Seizing the fields that they covet,
they take over houses as well,
owner and house they confiscate together,
taking both man and inheritance [Mic. 2:1-2].[15]

d. The Sabbath Day:

For six days you shall do your work, but stop on the seventh
day, so that your ox and your donkey may rest and the son of
your slave girl have a breathing space, and the stranger too
[Exod. 23:12].

The Sabbath was not only a religious interlude. It also had social
implications, for on that day the Israelite—in order to avoid social discrimination—permitted the animals and the slaves to enjoy a day of rest, thereby allowing for an equalization of work
and rest among all the people. The provision did not of course
assure a unification of classes, but it did act as a means of awakening the Israelites to certain social injustices.

The Exodus and the Agricultural Celebrations

Although Israel was predominantly a nomadic people, when
the Israelites entered the land of Canaan they encountered a series
of agricultural festivals that subsequently became a part of their
own social and religious system. The unique feature of the Jewish
observances, however, was the fact that these cosmological celebrations *became associated with the exodus, a historical event.*
The feast of unleavened bread, for example, was observed at the

beginning of the harvest season in the month of Abib, "the Month of the Ears of Corn," for this was the time when Yahweh had brought the Israelites "out of the land of Egypt" (Exod. 12:17, and 23:15). The time may well have been adopted by the Israelites from the Canaanite festival, "but since the week and the Sabbath are not found outside Israel, this feast must have taken on, apparently from the moment of its adoption, a strictly Israelite character"[16] and commemorated not only the beginning of the harvest but also the liberation from Egyptian bondage. By connecting the celebration to the worship of Yahweh who had brought the Israelites out of Egypt, the festival was purged of its idolatrous significance.

The time of the feast was important: as the Canaanite people ate bread made with the new harvest grain without utilizing leaven from a previous year's harvest in order to indicate that this was a new beginning,[17] Israel was obviously aware that its new beginning had already taken place (when Israel was still a child), and it would not have to begin anew each year with a harvest celebrating a new beginning. The Israelites knew that their beginning was situated in the past, and if they celebrated the agricultural feasts they did it with the knowledge that they had their own history. The feast of unleavened bread can be called a celebration of absolute discontinuity (which is precisely the eternal beginning) only when it is connected to the history of the people, and primordially to the exodus. Only so can it represent a continuation of a history already begun. The Israelites were aware of this and therefore of the unity of their time and of their history.

The agricultural celebrations were not, therefore, attacked or prohibited. They were neither suppressed nor abolished. Rather they were incorporated into Israelite history. The Israelites' contribution to the agriculturalists, whose work inclined them to begin with a new beginning at each harvest season, was a historical awareness: awareness of the past as united with the present.

Cultic Unity and Tribal Unity

The fundamental process of unifying the tribes of Israel always had as its axis the various sanctuaries. Shechem was the location of the first tribal convocation called by Joshua (Josh. 24:1). Then the entire community of the Israelites assembled at Shiloh (Josh. 18:1), where at one time the ark of the covenant was maintained, and subsequently national unity was consolidated by the placing of the ark in Jerusalem and the constructing of the temple. This was the period when Israel reached its zenith as a nation. *The progressive unification of the tribes, therefore, was accompanied by the progressive unification of cult,* which prepared the way for the emergence of monotheism:

> Thus says Israel's king
> and his redeemer, Yahweh Sabaoth:
> I am the first and the last;
> there is no other God besides me [Isa. 44:6].

Likewise, the division of the tribes resulted in religious divisions. The political division which took place when the northern tribes seceded after the death of Solomon was followed and perpetuated by a religious schism[18]—although in this case the Israelites did not relapse into the Canaanite cults. Jeroboam maintained his faith in Yahweh, but "he made two golden calves" and placed them in rival sanctuaries in order to prevent or discourage the people from going to the temple in Jerusalem to offer sacrifices (1 Kings 12:28), for he feared that such pilgrimages would incline the people toward a renewed subservience to Rehoboam, the king of Judah (1 Kings 12:27). The later division between the Samaritans and the Jews—which is alluded to in John 4:9—also led to religious antipathy and differences.

During the final phase of the development of official, codified cult, worship was prescribed for the temple in Jerusalem only, and all the other "high places" were definitively condemned. Consequently, when Israel was taken into exile, the people logically assumed that they had no place of worship. There were repeated attempts to reconstruct the original temple, but following the destruction of Jerusalem A.D. 70, the Jews were without an altar or place of sacrifice. It can be said with some assuredness that Israel learned through the Exile and its prolonged sufferings that true sacrifice was a contrite and humble heart and that this oblation was more significant than any other offering.

"With that gift shall I come into Yahweh's presence
and bow down before God on high?
Shall I come with holocausts,
with calves one year old?
Will he be pleased with rams by the thousand,
with libations of oil in torrents?
Must I give my firstborn for what I have done wrong,
the fruit of my body for my own sin?"
What is good has been explained to you, man;
this is what Yahweh asks of you:
only this, to act justly,
to love tenderly
and to walk humbly with your God [Mic. 6:6-8].

The Prophets' Criticism of Worship

According to Claude Tresmontant, "From the time of Amos,
the Hebrew prophets initiated criticism of the Israelite religion."[19]
This had become seriously contaminated by Canaanite worship
and was in danger of being overwhelmed by paganism.

Note the following examples:

I hate and despise your feasts,
I take no pleasure in your solemn festivals.
When you offer me holocausts, . . .
I reject your oblations,
and refuse to look at your sacrifices of fattened cattle
                                                    [Amos 5:21-22].

Fasting like yours today
will never make your voice heard on high.
Is that the sort of fast that pleases me,
a truly penitential day for men?
Hanging your head like a reed,
lying down on sackcloth and ashes?
Is that what you call fasting,
a day acceptable to Yahweh?
Is not this the sort of fast that pleases me
—it is the Lord Yahweh who speaks—
to break unjust fetters and undo the thongs of the yoke,

to let the oppressed go free,
and break every yoke,
to share your bread with the hungry,
and shelter the homeless poor,
to clothe the man you see to be naked
and not turn from your own kin?
Then will your light shine like the dawn
and your wound be quickly healed over [Isa. 58:4b–8].

Tresmontant comments:

The criticism leveled by the prophets against the Israelite
religion was essentially the censure of the old Canaanite ru-
diment of the magico-sacrificial pagan ritual contained in
the religion practiced by Israel. The transition from a religion based on a sacrificial system to one based on personal
faith—open to the knowledge of God whose fundamental
demand is for justice—moved toward a progressive realiza-
tion under the influence of the prophets of Israel.[20]

Three fundamental ideas constitute the prophets' basic criticisms of worship:

1. Its disconnection with history, seen on the occasions when a
rite was celebrated as something floating in history without either
reflecting it or questioning it.

2. Its passive coexistence with injustice, as can be inferred
from the texts cited above, along with many others.

3. Its magical character, as in the belief that by the mere ampu-
tation of the foreskin a relationship with Yahweh would be en-
sured. When the prophets spoke of "the circumcision of the
heart" (Jer. 4:4 and Deut. 10:16), they were insisting on the commitment of the person, and in this sense "demagicalization" cor-
responds to the growing personalization of the cult.

Conclusions

Upon completing the review of the more outstanding characteristics of religious cult in Israel, we can summarize them as follows:

1. We discover at the beginning a rupture with a people, a reli-

gion, and a cult as the indispensable condition for beginning the new process.

2. In the first syncretistic phase, the Israelites utilized the Canaanite sanctuaries and adapted them in order that the God of Israel would have a place among the other gods.

3. The sanctuaries were then converted into depositories of the historical exploits of their ancestors.

4. Beginning with the exodus Israel created a new ritual modality as the rites were converted into the cultual objectification of history and into historico-political reactivators.

5. The cultual objectification of the experience of the exodus, "the central event around which the Hebrews organized their total perception of reality," as Harvey Cox expresses it, favored or determined the mind of the people (its characterization) and the continual renourishment of their faith.

6. During the time of the conquest, they dislodged the Canaanites and expropriated their territory, their values, and their gods.

7. Israel was conscious of the incompatibility of the Canaanites' historical designs with the inhumane practices (sacred prostitution, the immolation of infants, etc.), and this awareness had a perceptible repercussion in the development of their own religious rites.

8. Civico-religious festivals were established in which social distinctions were made clear and challenges for justice were enunciated.

9. The agricultural festivals were not the wrong approach in regard to the constituent political reference of the people, for they injected a historical consciousness into the minds of the Israelite agriculturalists and cleansed the pagan festivals of idolatry.

10. The progressive unification of the nation was accompanied by a progressive unification of religious cult.

11. Finally, the prophets attacked the bifurcation of history and cult and its passive coexistence with injustice. At the same time, there was a demagicalization and a personalization with a strong social emphasis.

This brief analysis allows us to conclude as follows:

1. Geographical and historical contextualization by the Meso-

potamian and Canaanite peoples (religions) in whose womb was formed the religion of Israel was closely related to the Semitic religions (continuity), but the Israelite cult had its own personality, resulting from a progressive characterization of itself and of its God gained in the historical conflict with those religions (discontinuity).

2. The Israelites, nevertheless, did not produce their religion by "spontaneous generation" or in a mechanistic way. Rather it was the interpretation of their own historical experiences that forced a reinterpretation of the traditional religious forms. It was their new historical consciousness that determined their religious modality. For this reason it would be better to say that the religion of Israel was not formed for them (as if something had appeared without a historical subject), but rather that they formed it. Who? The patriarchs, the judges, the priests, the people of Israel themselves. They developed their religion, but according to conditions that they did not select—namely, in the Semitic matrix.

3. The religion of Israel was therefore engendered actively and conflictually because it was born, not in spite of humanity, but because of humanity in the struggles with other peoples and other religions. Like all historical phenomena, it was not the result simply of human volition; it resulted from the response of human volition to something presented to it—the Semitic sociocultural context. It was not simply what human beings *wanted to do;* it was what they *could do* in their de facto contextualization.

4. Among all these discontinuities one that may be called *qualitative* should be highlighted. During the patriarchal era it consisted in associating the deeds of Israel's ancestors with the sanctuaries. After the Exile it consisted in cultually objectifying history in order to celebrate it as a historical exploit of God and the people in a mobile form.

CHAPTER TWO

The Passage from the Rite of Israel to the Christian Rite (Reinterpretation II)

> *To celebrate the Eucharist is to endorse the act of the Father who radically negated the injustice by which the sin of the world victimized the Just One.*

The Political Context of the Life of Jesus

In order to understand Jesus' criticism of the cultic forms of his day and the significance of the passover that he celebrated with his disciples, it is necessary to consider first the socio-political framework in which his life developed and the growing conflict that he caused. The discussion here will be limited, however, to the principal milestones in his life. No exhaustive study—though various efforts have been made—has yet been achieved.

As the writer of the Gospel of Luke indicates in his reference to the census ordered by Caesar Augustus, Jesus was born at the time when Judea was about to become officially an occupied province of the Roman Empire (Luke 2:1-2; 3:1-2), a time when

Jewish nationalism, especially as represented by the Zealots, was conspiring to liberate the nation from Roman domination. The failure of the effort made by Judas the Galilean is noted by Luke (Acts 5:36–37), and there are subsequent references to at least two other political uprisings: the bloody repression by Pilate of the rebellious Galileans (Luke 13:1) and likewise Mark's reference to Barabbas as one of those "rioters who had committed murder during an uprising" (15:7). The two robbers who were crucified with Jesus were also probably put to death for political reasons.

This political background and particular environment of messianic expectation, common to the different socio-religious currents of the era (Sadducees, Pharisees, Essenes, and Zealots), constituted the environment in which Jesus lived.[1] Jesus moved with the intelligence that was his, indicating agreement with some facets of society, differences with and criticisms of others, without evading the commitments or the consequences that those positions implied.

On the one hand he challenged Herod, who attempted to intimidate him (Luke 13:31), and on the other Jesus confronted the Pharisees and scribes who had devised a scheme whereby obligations to parents could be evaded by children who declared that their resources were dedicated to the temple (Matt. 15:3–7). The beneficiaries of such a maneuver were obvious, as well as the reason why they resented so intensely Jesus' criticism. Jesus described these religious leaders as "the blind leading the blind" because they contended that the eating of certain foods could make a person impure (Matt. 15:10–14). He condemned their hypocrisy and reproached them openly because of the injustices that the people were suffering (Matt. 23 and Luke 37). He warned his disciples to beware of the "leaven" of the Pharisees (Matt. 16:6), and even questioned their authority to pose as religious leaders of the people:

> The scribes and the Pharisees occupy the chair of Moses. You must therefore do what they tell you and listen to what they say; but do not be guided by what they do: since they do not practice what they preach. They tie up heavy burdens and lay them on men's shoulders, but will they lift a finger to move them? Not they! Everything they do is done to attract

attention, like wearing broader phylacteries and longer tassels, like wanting to take the place of honor at banquets and the front seats in the synagogues, being greeted obsequiously in the market square and having people call them Rabbi [Matt. 23:1-7].

His criticism and warnings were so clear and evident that he soon gained the confidence of the people who followed him in multitudes "because he taught them with authority, and not like their own scribes" (Matt. 7:20), to the point that the people began to ask if "when the Christ comes, will he give more signs than this man?" (John 7:31).

Many who listened to Jesus declared, "Surely he must be the prophet," while others asserted, "He is the Christ" (John 7:40, 41). Obviously there was not a consensus in regard to who Jesus was, but his impact was sufficient to intrigue and fascinate his contemporaries: "the people could not agree about him" (John 7:43).

It is evident, therefore, why the power brokers were alarmed because of the growing popularity Jesus enjoyed among the people and why they attacked him and "tried to force answers from him on innumerable questions, setting traps to catch him out in something he might say" (Luke 11:54).

Their fear of him was so great that they attempted again and again to trip him up with questions and dilemmas such as those regarding adultery or paying taxes to the Roman government. His response to the latter question was expected to establish him as a nationalist or as a collaborator who was soft on the Roman occupation. The culmination of all these attempts to ensnare him is clearly indicated by Luke, who says that the religio-political leaders sent spies who feigned sincerity in order to entangle and expose Jesus as someone plotting insurrection (Luke 20:2-8, 20-26).

These conspiracies and traps failed, however, and the popularity of Jesus with the people increased so alarmingly that the religious leaders agreed "to expel from the synagogue anyone who should acknowledge Jesus as the Christ" (John 9:23). There were, nonetheless, those—even among the leaders—"who did believe in him . . . but they did not admit it, through fear of the Pharisees and fear of being expelled from the synagogue" (John 12:42). The chief priests went so far as to agree "to kill Lazarus as well, since it was on his account that many of the Jews were leaving them and believing in Jesus" (John 12:10–11).

When the temple guards were sent by the chief priests and Pharisees to arrest Jesus and they returned without him, they were asked, "Why haven't you brought him in?" The guards replied, "There has never been anybody who has spoken like him" (John 7:46)—evidently indicating their fear of the masses. The religious leaders were infuriated and sarcastically reproached them saying, "So, you have been led astray as well? Have any of the authorities believed in him? Any of the Pharisees?" (John 7:47–48). Exasperated, the chief priests and the Pharisees declared—quite sure of their own theology—"This rabble knows nothing about the law; they are damned" (John 7:49). In other words, these plebeians, these common folk, know nothing about God's law.

The growing conflict between Jesus and the religious authorities reached its apogee, and the intensity of the dispute made the situation more and more intolerable for those who saw themselves as responsible for the maintenance of public order, whereupon consideration was given to the possibility of eliminating Jesus. "The chief priests and the scribes, with the support of the leading citizens, tried to do away with him, but they did not see how they could carry this out because the people as a whole hung on his words" (Luke 19:48). According to the Gospel of John, from the day of the resurrection of Lazarus, the authorities "were determined" to put Jesus to death (11:53).

Jesus' triumphal entry into Jerusalem and the succeeding collision with the temple authorities led to the denouement, for when he entered Jerusalem there was a great public manifestation as the people acclaimed him king. The Pharisees were scandalized and demanded that Jesus reproach the people for their outbursts. Jesus refused, saying, "I tell you, if these keep silence the stones will cry out" (Luke 19:40).

Then entering the temple he drove out those who were buying, selling, trading, and exchanging money, upsetting "the tables of the moneychangers and the chairs of those who were selling pigeons, and declaring, 'According to Scripture, . . . my house will be called a house of prayer, but you are turning it into a robbers' den' " (Matt. 21:12–13).[2] It would be a mistake to equate what was going on in Jerusalem under the guise of religious necessity with merchants and entrepreneurs of our day. The temple was the center of the financial operations of Israel, and those who did business there were the elite of the nation and the members of the families of the priests, users of their treasuries and of the income from the sale of animals brought as "offerings." What is described, therefore, is an open collision between Jesus and the power structure of the day, and it is not surprising that the Pharisees interpreted the situation as desperate: "You see, there is nothing you can do; look, the whole world is running after him!" (John 12:19).

A meeting of the Jewish leaders was seen as imperative, and "the chief priests and Pharisees called a meeting. 'Here is this man working all these signs,' they said, 'and what action are we taking? If we let him go on in this way everybody will believe in him, and the Romans will come and destroy the Holy Place and our nation' " (John 11:47–48). The religio-political leaders of Israel were quite aware of the danger implicit for the nation in permitting the people to proclaim as king one such as Jesus of Nazareth. It would be an open affront to the Roman empire and Caesar. Moreover, these leaders were not at all inclined to lose their power and control over the people. Caiaphas, a loyal agent of the empire who had been named by Valerius Maximus, suggested a logical solution to the dilemma: "You don't seem to have grasped the situation at all; you fail to see that it is better for one man to die for the people, than for the whole nation to be destroyed" (John 11:50). It was not necessary to spell out in detail the implications of this "solution" because everyone knew who would be the "sacrificial lamb."

From that day, therefore, the religious leaders were *"determined"* to silence Jesus, and they *"made plans* to arrest Jesus by some trick and have him put to death. They said, however, 'it must not be during the festivities; there must be no disturbance among the people' " (Matt. 26:4–5). We have italicized the "determined" and the "made plans" in order that the reader will not miss the fact that the persons responsible for the decision and the death of Jesus were the leaders, the *power groups* or *upper classes* of Israel. *It was not the people.* It is a mistake, therefore, to argue that the "will of the people," which at first in great multitudes acclaimed Jesus as king, suddenly turned against him and demanded his crucifixion. The decision to eliminate Jesus was made by the ruling classes, and its implementation—which we shall now discuss—will prove it.

What is the scriptural evidence regarding the implementation? In the first place there was a "fifth column" among Jesus' own disciples, one who sold him out for thirty pieces of silver (Matt. 26:15). This same Judas led the police to where they would find Jesus during the night in order that his arrest would not cause a commotion among the people. Then, despite the fact that "several lying witnesses came forward," the chief priests and the whole Sanhedrin searched frantically for other "evidence against Jesus . . . on which they might pass the death sentence" (Matt. 26:59). It should be remembered that those considering Jesus' case had already decided to put him to death. When the Roman governor Pilate sought to exonerate Jesus and release him, "the chief priests and the elders . . . had already persuaded the crowd to demand the release of Barabbas and the execution of Jesus" (Matt. 27:20), thereby making it appear that it was the people who really desired Jesus' death. The writer of John's Gospel, however, points out that it was the chief priests and the guards who began shouting, "Crucify him! Crucify him!" (John: 19:6). These same religious leaders perceived the vacillation of the governor, and when he insisted that he found no basis on which to condemn Jesus (John 19:4), they shouted, "If you set him free you are no friend of Caesar's; anyone who makes himself king is defying Caesar" (John 19:12).

Though governor, Pilate evidently sat uneasily on his throne, and he was unwilling to risk the charge of disloyalty. There is a note of sarcasm in his words to the leaders: "Do you want me to crucify your king?" But the chief priests responded, "We have no king except Caesar" (John 19:16). The placard, then, that Pilate ordered written and affixed to the cross, "Jesus the Nazarene, King of the Jews," served a dual purpose. It provided a public political justification for the execution, and likewise it allowed the governor to mock sardonically the Jewish leaders. They protested immediately and asked Pilate to revise the words that had been written in Hebrew, Latin, and Greek. They wanted the notice to read, "This man said: I am King of the Jews." But Pilate was adamant, declaring that what he had written, "King of the Jews" in Hebrew, Latin, and Greek, was there to stay. "What I have written, I have written," he said (John 19:22).

The implementation of the plan was accomplished, but after the resurrection of Jesus a new scheme had to be concocted, and it required an additional bribe. The Matthean account is as follows:

> While they were on their way, some of the guards went off into the city to tell the chief priests all that happened. These held a meeting with the elders and, after some discussion, handed a considerable sum of money to the soldiers with these instructions. "This is what you must say, 'His disciples came during the night and stole him away while we were asleep.' And should the governor come to hear of this, we undertake to put things right with him ourselves and to see that you do not get into trouble." The soldiers took the money and carried out their instructions [28:11-15].

News of the resurrection constituted for the religious leaders a new political danger, and it explains their anxiety and the seeming necessity to invest money in continued subornation. Still another indication of the political explosiveness of the resurrection of Jesus can be noted in the warnings issued by the Sanhedrin to the disciples to desist even from mentioning the name of Jesus in their preaching. "We gave you a formal warning . . . not to preach in this name, and what have you done? You have filled Jerusalem with your teaching, and seem determined to fix the guilt of this man's death on us" (Acts 5:28). When the apostle Peter responded that loyalty to God took precedence over loyalty to government, the authorities were incensed to the point that they were ready to execute the apostles (Acts 5:33). This continued confrontation between the disciples and the government finally resulted in the execution of Stephen (Acts 7), whose death was followed by intensified persecution of the church in Jerusalem (Acts 8:1-3).

Jesus' Critique of Cultism

This political context that we have just described serves as a backdrop for analyzing the more specific references of Jesus to the cultism of his era. He took upon himself the prophetic criticism of cultism and even surpassed it by insisting that he did not come to abolish the law or the prophets but to complete them—that is, to give them meaning (Matt. 5:17). But this does not imply that his words are a mere repetition of what the prophets had said, for he declared that one does not put new wine in old wineskins or sew a new piece of cloth on an old suit (Matt. 9:16–17). Jesus followed the direction of the prophets and affirmed their legacy, but his contribution centered on his critique of worship—which had lost contact with its historical roots and responsibility—and on his emphasis on its anthropological significance, dissolving its anthropocentric character entirely.

He began by attacking the formalism and verbosity of the prayers of the Pharisees (Matt. 6:7), and he placed above the worship of words the *worship of praxis:*

> It is not those who say to me, "Lord, Lord," who will enter the kingdom of heaven, but the person who does the will of my Father in heaven [Matt. 7:21].

The crucial element in religion, he insisted, is not words but deeds. What a person does and not what a person says is the definitive basis for entering the kingdom. The history that each one forges is the authentic cult they offer (note that I am not saying "the *best* cult"), and in history one worships or does not worship God. Paul wrote to the church at Rome, "Think of God's mercy, my brothers, and worship him, I beg you, in a way that is worthy of thinking beings, by offering your living bodies as a holy sacrifice, truly pleasing to God" (12:1).

Faithful to the social implications that the Old Testament had attributed to the Sabbath—and in order to divest it of magical and superstitious traditions—Jesus practiced mercy and justice even on this day. And to those who criticized him he retorted that they had not learned the significance of the prophetic demand or the meaning of the words, "What I want is mercy, not sacrifice" (Hos. 6:6; Matt. 9:13 and 12:7). Stripping the Sabbath of its magico-cosmological traces and converting it openly to a day for humanity, Jesus declared, "A human being is far more important than a sheep," and, one might add, more important than the day itself (Matt. 12:12). For, he said, "the Sabbath was made for man, not man for the Sabbath" (Mark 2:27), thereby affirming his own lordship over the Sabbath (Matt. 12:8). The Sabbath, he implied, is best celebrated in the practice of mercy and justice.

Emphasizing fellowship as the indispensable precondition for making an offering, Jesus declared, "So then, if you are bringing your offering to the altar and there remember that your brother has something against you, leave your offering there before the altar, go and be reconciled with your brother first, and then come back and present your offering" (Matt. 5:23-24). And he emphatically condemned the "tradition" or practice whereby children could evade their responsibility to the needs of their parents by making a promisory offering to the temple of what should be utilized in giving aid and succor to their aged and needy parents (Matt. 15:1-9). Jesus is especially harsh about the ways in which the scribes and Pharisees had permitted and even capitalized on this kind of hypocrisy and irresponsibility. In one case after another Jesus makes crystal clear that the important thing is not the offering itself (the phenomenon) but rather the human action that precedes it and thus qualifies it (that is, the act behind the phenomenon). The practice of those who were making offerings was what counted, and for this reason the fruits of injustice could not be received as offerings.[3]

For this same reason Jesus rejected the idea that a thing can be classified as pure or impure independent of the act of the person. Even less could the person be classified as pure or impure, for what goes into the mouth does not make a person unclean; it is what comes out of the mouth that makes one unclean. . . . But the things that come out of the mouth come from the heart, and it is these that make one unclean. For from the heart come evil intentions: murder, adultery, fornication, theft, perjury, slander. These are the things that make a man unclean (Matt. 15:19-20). It is the person, not things, who is responsible for evil. It is the person who makes things pure or impure.

Finally, Jesus criticized severely those who took pride in the fulfillment of religious trivialities but ignored "the weightier matters of the law—justice, mercy, good faith!" (Matt. 23:23).

The Paschal Content of the Sufferings of Jesus

There is no doubt that Jesus celebrated his own suffering in the context of the Jewish passover and that during the celebration he followed the traditional ritual, serving the elements with the words and liturgical gestures common in that observance.[4]

Matthew's narration indicates that "on the first day of Unleavened Bread the disciples came to Jesus and said, 'Where do you want us to make the preparations for you to eat the Passover?' " (Matt. 26:17), and that Jesus had already intimated that it would be during the passover celebration that he would be "handed over to be crucified" (26:2). He indicated to them that he desired greatly to eat the passover with them: "I have longed to eat this passover with you before I suffer; because, I tell you, I shall not eat it again until it is fulfilled in the kingdom of God" (Luke 22:16).

The historical setting of the passover meal is therefore clear. The texts refer to "the preparations that the disciples thought needed to be made" (Matt: 26:17), and that when Jesus "was at the table with the twelve disciples" (Matt. 26:20) and while they were eating, Judas "dipped his hand into the dish" (20:23). One can reasonably suppose that besides including the paschal lamb, the meal consisted also of the bitter herbs—eaten to remind the faithful of the suffering and oppression of the Israelites during the time of slavery—the unleavened bread and the cups of blessing. Luke suggests that they drank from the cup on two occasions (22:17, 20). These last two courses of the meal were customarily blessed by the father of the family when he took them in his hands and gave thanks (Luke 22:17, 19).[5] It is evident that Jesus introduced some variations at this point. The synoptic writers indicate that following the celebration, the disciples also sang a hymn (Matt. 26:30) and with this they concluded the passover meal.

The writer of John's Gospel adds an incident that is not recorded in the synoptics—namely, that during the passover supper Jesus washed the feet of the disciples (John 13:1ff.), a symbolic act, which, in context, is an explanation of his own passover and a manifestation of his understanding of it.

From John's Gospel one can also infer that the historical occasion of this event was the celebration of the passover, although the writer concentrates his attention primarily on the death of Jesus and not on the supper as such. The writer alludes to the passover context three times, first when he says "it was the passover Preparation Day" when Jesus was condemned (19:14). Again he says, "It was "Preparation Day," when Jesus' body was removed from the Cross (19:31). Finally, he states that "it was the Jewish Day of Preparation" when Jesus' corpse was placed in the tomb (19:42).

In the mind of the writer of John, the preparation for the passion of Jesus was contextualized by the preparation for the passover. Jesus was the paschal lamb whose bones could not be broken (Exod. 12:46), a typical example of reinterpretation. The Jews, without knowing it, were preparing the authentic passover. Jesus was the paschal lamb, according to the Gospel of John (1:29), and Paul elaborates on the theme even more when he says, "Christ, our passover, has been sacrificed" (1 Cor. 5:7).

The passover in its totality brings with it the memory of the liberation from Egyptian slavery, but it also suggests the great liberation that will be realized with the coming of the Messiah. A prayer said at the passover supper implored that God would send the Messiah, whose coming would take place on a night similar to the one when Yahweh struck down the firstborn of the Egyptians (Exod. 12:29).[6] The night of the passover became the time when the Jews expected the Messiah; it was the night when he would surely come.[7] Perhaps for this reason the writer of John remembered that when Judas went out, it was night: "When Judas went out, night had fallen" (John 13:30). "This is the night . . ." the church would later declare.

Jesus, therefore, did not reject or nullify the rite of the passover, for he *did not come to abolish it* but rather to give it meaning. Jesus celebrated the passover with his disciples, and in so doing celebrated also the liberation of his people: The Eucharist can be understood in its most profound sense only against the liturgical tradition of the Old Testament. The worst misunderstandings would arise from any attempt to understand the eucharistic meal as an entirely new and independent act by Christ.[8] "From the passover, by way of the Eucharist, to the messianic banquet, there is a continuity, an analogy, a unity, even if the rite becomes externally modified."[9] But Jesus injects into the passover of his people a new meaning. He did not come to abolish *but rather to give meaning*, and he incorporates and adds to the rite, with wondrous simplicity and freedom, variations that, insist the evangelists, make the messianic meal unique. The evangelists and Paul have not recorded all the symbols and words used by Jesus, but only those that emphasize what is new in the traditional ritual.[10] To these (gestures and words) we will refer now in view of the fact that they constitute a *discontinuity* and Jesus' own contribution.

The Blood to Be Shed

At the time of the supper the preoccupation in the heart of Jesus was the imminence of what he called "his hour." It is the anguish of one who knows himself to be a marked man. But his desire is not to "institute" or "legislate," but rather to attempt a single act: to indicate the relation between what is taking place—his historically foreseeable denouement—with the passover.

In the context of the supper, Jesus takes a cup and says, "Take this and share it among you, because from now on, I tell you, I shall not drink wine until the kingdom of God comes" (Luke 22:17). He is obviously referring to the image of the vine already utilized by the prophets (Jer. 2:21 and Isa. 5:1). Jeremiah had reproved Israel for having become a "degenerate plant," a "bastard vine" (Jer. 2:21). Now Jesus declares himself to be the "true vine" (John 15:1). The remnant of Israel comprises new "branches" (John 15:5). The wine, a product of the vine—remember that Jesus at the time probably held the cup in his hand or at least had it placed before him—is related now by means of his prophetic gesture to the blood that is about to be shed (Luke 22:20). There where the oil was squeezed from the olives (Luke 22:29)—namely, Gethsemane (Matt. 26:36) signifying the winepress—there will be the initial pressing of the "true vine," and finally there will be the cross (John 20:34). His blood—the true product of the *vine* (which is himself) and which he resists "drinking" (Luke 22:42 and Matt. 26:39, 42)—is the new "wine."

Jesus had himself said that "unless a wheat grain falls on the ground and dies, it remains only a single grain" (John 12:24). He knew further that the "wicked husbandmen" would have no respect for the owner's son (Luke 20:9, 19), that the winepress would be crimson (Isa. 63:1–6) with the "blood of the grapes" (Gen. 49:11 and Deut. 32:14), and that they would press and trample upon the "product of the vine."

The gestures—more than the words—that Jesus used to connect the passover to his "hour" will be fully understood in the

postpaschal situation in the light of complementary episodes—
e.g., the discourse on bread (John 6:32–58). Besert notes:

> They will, however, definitely hold on to his unexpected ac-
> tion in the course of the meal. They will make the connec-
> tion between the liberation from Egypt and the expected
> liberator. They will understand that, in his own body and in
> his blood shed in fidelity to his mission, Jesus is actually
> accomplishing what the immolated lamb of the passover rite
> could only symbolize.[11]

His gesture, moreover, linked his figure to that of Moses, the liberator of old, to the covenant, to which Jesus explicitly refers, to
the departure from Egypt, and to the blood of Sinai. A new exodus was in gestation.

In the mind of Jesus the imminence of his hour apparently is
directly related to the imminence of the kingdom. *The hour of
Christ is the hour of the kingdom.* The Father confers the
kingdom on Jesus, and he in turn confers it upon his disciples
(Luke 22:28–30). He will not eat the passover "until it is fulfilled
in the kingdom of God" (Luke 22:16). He will "not drink wine
until the kingdom of God comes," (Luke 22:18) or "until the day I
drink the new wine with you in the kingdom of my Father" (Matt.
26:29). What then is this day when Jesus will eat his passover and
drink his wine? We can deduce the answer from Mark 10:38–39,
when James and John said to him, "Allow us to sit one at your
right hand and the other at your left hand in your glory" (Mark
10:38). And Jesus responded, "You do not know what you are
asking. Can you drink the cup which I must drink, or be baptized
with the baptism with which I must be baptized?" (10:38). It is the
day of the Lord, the day when he will pass from this world to the
Father—or as John's Gospel expresses it, "from death to life." It
is the inauguration day of the kingdom. The Father, therefore,
manifests solidarity with the efforts of the people who wanted to
make Jesus king (John 12:12–15) and with the vocation of him
who had been born for this (John 18:37). There is an unexpected
reversal. The new king is enthroned on a cross, and his enthrone-
ment is proclaimed in Hebrew, Latin, and Greek (John 19:20).

The Body to Be Given

Although the gesture of the blood (wine) spilled by the "wicked tenant farmers" (Luke 20:9–19) indicates the socio-political context of the suffering and death of Christ, it is the bread above all that signifies this context most explicitly. "Now as they were eating, Jesus took some bread, and when he had said the blessing he broke it and gave it to his disciples. 'Take it and eat,' he said, 'this is my body' " (Matt. 26:26).

"This is my body *which will be given for you*" (Luke 22:19). Or as the Apostle Paul expressed it, "For this is what I received from the Lord, and in turn passed on to you: that on the same night that he was betrayed, the Lord Jesus took some bread, and thanked God for it and broke it, and he said, 'This is my body, which is for you; do this as a memorial of me' " (1 Cor. 11:23–24).

One may infer therefore that the context of this prophetic and premonitory gesture (which, as we will see, constituted the prophetic setting in Israel) *is unquestionably* the *historico-political context of the betrayal* (*traditio* in Latin, *traición* in Spanish). It is not merely a liturgical context.[12]

The Betrayal by Judas

"The Son of Man will be delivered into the hands of men" (Mark 9:31).

"The Son of Man is about to be handed over to the chief priests and the scribes" (Mark 10:33).

"The chief priests and the scribes were looking for some way of doing away with him, because they mistrusted the people" (Luke 22:2). "The chief priests and the elders of the people assembled in the palace of the high priest, whose name was Caiaphas, and made plans to arrest Jesus by some trick and have him put to death. They said, however, 'It must not be during the festivities; there must be no disturbance among the people' " (Matt. 26: 3–5).

Judas Iscariot therefore went to the chief priests and said to them, "What are you prepared to give me if I hand him over to you?" (Matt. 26:15).

Accepting the bribe, Judas "looked for an opportunity to betray him to them" (Luke 22:6).

"Judas the traitor knew the place well, since Jesus had often met with his disciples there, and he brought the cohort to this place together with a detachment of guards sent by the chief priests and the Pharisees, all with lanterns and torches and weapons" (John 18:2–3).

"It will be passover, as you know, in two days' time, and the Son of Man will be handed over to be crucified" (Matt. 26:2). "Judas the traitor was standing among them" (John 18:5).

"Jesus was troubled in spirit and declared, 'I tell you most solemnly, one of you will betray me' " (John 13:21).

The following texts relate the betrayal to the supper:

> When evening came he was at table with the twelve disciples. And *while they were eating* he said, "I tell you solemnly, one of you *is about to betray me*." . . . "Someone, who has dipped his hand into the dish with me, will betray me. . . . alas for that man by whom the Son of Man is betrayed! Better for that man if he had never been born!" Judas, who was to betray him, asked in his turn, "Not I, Rabbi, surely?" "They are your own words," answered Jesus. Now *as they were eating,* Jesus took some bread, and when he had said the blessing he broke it and gave it to the disciples. "Take it and eat," he said, "this is my body" [Matt. 26:20–26].

> Then he took some bread and when he had given thanks, broke it and gave it to them, saying, "This is my body *which will be given* for you; do this as a memorial of me" [Luke 22:19].

> *They were at supper,* and the devil had already put it into the mind of Judas Iscariot, son of Simon, *to betray him* [John 13:2].

A few moments before he was arrested Jesus said, "Now the hour has come when the Son of Man *is to be betrayed* into the hands of sinners. Get up! Let us go! *My betrayer* is already close at hand" (Matt. 26:45–46).

During the act of betrayal, "Judas, one of the Twelve . . . went up to Jesus to kiss him. Jesus said, 'Judas, are you betraying the Son of Man with a kiss?' " (Luke 22:47–48).

The Betrayal by the Chief Priests

"Now we are going up to Jerusalem, and the Son of Man is about to be handed over to the chief priests and the scribes. They will condemn him to death and *will hand him over* to the pagans, who will mock him and spit at him and scourge him and put him to death; and after three days he will rise again" (Mark 10:33–34).

"Then taking the Twelve aside he said to them, 'Now we are going up to Jerusalem, and everything that is written by the prophets about the Son of Man is to come true. For he *will be handed over* to the pagans and will be mocked, maltreated and spat on' " (Luke 18:31–32). One should remember at this point that the Gospel of Luke was directed especially to the Gentiles or pagans.

"If he were not a criminal, we should not be *handing him over* to you" (John 18:30).

" 'It is your own people and the chief priests who *have handed you over* to me,' Pilate said" (John 18:35).

Jesus in the same act in which the people betrayed him (*traditum est*), was handed over (*traditum est*) to the Gentiles (Mark 10:33). Origen would later remark that in turning Jesus over to the Roman authorities, the Jewish leaders were handing over "on a platter" their *autobasileia* (their limited self-government) to the Gentiles. They were in effect committing political and juridical suicide. "The one who handed me over to you has the greater guilt," Jesus said (John 19:11).

Conclusion

Matthew, Mark, Luke, John, and Paul all state explicitly and with insistence (not in passing) the relationship of the prophetic gesture of the bread with the socio-political context. We may say, therefore, that the symbol of the bread is determined by the historical act of being handed over or betrayed, which it symbolizes. The words, "This is my body that is given for you," summarize, or better said, ultra-summarize, the complexity of the historico-political event, which is referred to as the "memorial" of the death of the Lord.

Given the "obstinacy" of the scripture writers in indicating the relationship between the symbol and the political context (we have mentioned twenty texts), which, we repeat, is summarized in the words "to be handed over," it is difficult to explain the many mystifying theological lines constructed around the death of Jesus as if it were a death resulting from natural causes and not the result of socio-political conflict. The cold fact is that he was betrayed (with the dual significance of being handed over and being betrayed) and was sentenced to die. He did not, however, die a natural death. Jesus was put to death.

Those who arbitrarily insist that Christ voluntarily gave himself up negate the true historicity of Christ. The actions to which John 18:4-8 allude are precisely the evidence that Jesus could have appealed to the Father and he would have placed at Jesus' disposition more than twelve legions of angels (Matt. 26:53). But he decided to "drink the cup that his Father had given him" (John 18:11). This indicates simply that Jesus decided to accept history—his historicity—with its ultimate consequences without appealing to his extraordinary powers for his personal protection, a decision consistent with his previous attitude toward power.

The Political Significance of the Death and Resurrection

Those who depoliticize the death of Jesus depoliticize also its counterpart: the resurrection. And we come back to where we started: all of theology is emasculated because it is supported by a single depoliticized point of departure.

Jesus did not die, but rather Jesus was put to death, and to put someone to death is an active negation of life. Correspondingly, the resurrection is an active negation of this prior active negation, and for this reason an active affirmation.

The resurrection is not simply germination or life emerging from death. Organismic and mechanistic theories fail completely on this point. How can death germinate or flower? The resurrection is not simply a power that burst forth because evil could not contain life either virtually, potentially, or incipiently in the negation of life. Much less could it be a product of itself, the segregation of itself, or simply change in itself. The resurrection is a *new creation*, and as such is the exclusive, salvific, and unparalleled act of God. It is the act by which the Father powerfully confronted death in order to snatch his Son from its clutches. It is the active negation of the death of Christ in order to re-create him.

For this reason it is not through death that we live, but by the active negation of death from which we march to life and the resurrection. It is not therefore by one's giving oneself passively or willingly to pain and to death that one comes to life. This was believed and unfortunately practiced by many ascetics. It is not a manichaeism of the body or a manichaeism of pleasure and of joy that are the way. They are dead-end streets. They are impasses.

Those who actively and energetically confront death and all its variants (pain, injustice, sin, and oppression) are actively collaborating with the power of the resurrection of God that was initiated in Jesus Christ. And this policy of negating the negation is the active prolongation of this power until its confirmation.

Jesus was not simply victorious over death as such, but victorious over death as a result of an injustice that compacted the magnitude of the sin of the world. Death is the result of sin, St. Paul tells us in Romans 5:12. Victory over death resulting from the ultimate paroxysm of sin was not achieved by the injustice done to some just one, but by the injustice done to *the* Just One. In that moment, therefore, when the sin of the world dealt its final blow, it was taken by assault and defeated completely. The Father thereby put to death (negation) death itself (negation) with the resurrection of his Son (affirmation). He thus negated the radical negation with an affirmation no less radical, an affirmation that is the foundation of our hope. He revealed the "execution" as injustice, unmasking it as the sin of the world, making Christ just and judging the world by it (John 16:8–11). He thus rebelled against the "justice" of the world.

By raising Jesus from the dead, "God showed that the one whom the law and the civilization controlled by the law condemned as impious was indeed just. For Paul this action of God is

God's supreme revelation. It is the revelation of the justice of God in absolute contrast with the justice of human civilization and law, in which sin has been incarnated."[13]

Thus, if Christ did not die a natural death, and if the resurrection is not simply victory over natural death, the Eucharist—the proclamation of the death of Christ—is not the proclamation of the natural death of Christ but of the socio-political injustice by which Christ was put to death. And if the Father did not raise Christ from natural death, but raised him who was "handed over and then disowned in the presence of Pilate after Pilate had decided to release him" (Acts 3:13), the Just One whom "you killed" (Acts 3:15), then the Eucharist is not the kerygmatic proclamation of the resurrection of one from natural death, but the resurrection of one from political injustice.

To celebrate the Eucharist, therefore, is to affirm the act by which the Father radically negated the injustice resulting from the sin of the world, and to proclaim publicly the injustice committed against the Just One, not simply that it may be exposed and denounced, but primarily to collaborate with the Father in the resurrection (affirmation) of those affected by injustice (negation).

The imperative of Christ to "do this as a memorial of me" (Luke 22:19 and 1 Cor. 11:24)—so often interpreted merely ritualistically—is not primarily a solicitation to repeat the rite but to repeat his handing over to the people, to which he alludes with his gestures or symbols. Rather, the passover has now been converted into a psycho-social memorial of the event that he is acting out and whose denouement is imminent.

Prophetic Warning Gestures

In order to understand the gestures of Jesus with the bread (which he broke and gave to each of the disciples) and the wine (which he poured and shared) we should remember the so-called symbolic acts of the prophets, which we prefer to call "prophetic premonitory gestures" and which, it may be said, are also premonitory mimes" (a kind of analysis of the situation). All of them occurred in very concrete historical situations, which, although they cannot be examined in detail in this context, nevertheless "dramatize" the foretold outcome.[14]

The prophet Ahijah "took the new cloak that he was wearing and tore it into twelve strips," and said to Jeroboam, "Take ten strips for yourself, for thus Yahweh speaks, the God of Israel, 'I am going to tear the kingdom from Solomon's hand and give ten tribes to you' " (1 Kings 11:29-31). Zedekiah made some iron horns, took them, and declared to Jehoshaphat, "With these you will gore the Aramaeans till you make an end of them" (1 Kings 22:11). Joash, the king of Israel, was told by Elisha to aim his bow and arrow toward the East saying, "Arrow of victory over Aram! You will defeat Aram at Aphek completely" (2 Kings 13:17). After the people made a promise to God in the presence of Nehemiah that they would make restitution for the exploitation of their kinsmen, the prophet shook out the lap of his gown with the words, "May God do this, and shake out of his house and property any man who does not keep this promise; may he be shaken out like this and left empty!" (Neh. 5:13). Jeremiah broke a clay pot before the people and declared, "Yahweh Sabaoth says this: I am going to break this people and this city just as one breaks a potter's pot, irreparably" (Jer. 19:10-11). On another occasion the prophet placed a yoke and rope on his neck and said, "The nation . . . that bends its neck to the king of Babylon and submits to him, I shall leave in peace on its own soil—it is Yahweh who speaks—to farm it and stay in it" (Jer. 27:11). Still a third time Jeremiah tied a stone to a book and had it thrown into the middle of the Euphrates with the words, "So shall Babylon sink, never again to rise from the disaster with which I am going to overwhelm her" (Jer. 51:64).

The prophet Ezekiel was told to shoulder his pack and go out like an exile in the evening—making sure that the people are watching—make a hole in the wall and go through it, and as the people observed, he was to go out into the dark. Then the following morning he was told to address the people and say, "The Lord Yahweh says this: 'This oracle is directed against Jerusalem and the whole House of Israel wherever they are living.' Say, 'I am a symbol for you; the thing I have done will be done to them; they will go into exile, into banishment.' Their ruler will shoulder his pack in the dark and go out through the wall; a hole will be made to let him out; he will cover his face rather than see the country . . . I shall take him to Babylon" (Ezek. 12:1-13). In Caesarea the prophet Agabus took the girdle of the Apostle Paul, tied up his own feet and hands, and said, "This is what the Holy Spirit says, 'The man this girdle belongs to will be bound like this by the Jews in Jerusalem, and handed over to the pagans' " (Acts 21:10-11).

The occasions cited above should evidence the fact that Jesus did not use an unusual or unknown "didactic method" that took the disciples by surprise. Rather his prophetic gesture had long-standing secular roots and was commonplace among the prophets. Jesus had done something of the same thing in cursing the fig tree (Mark 11:12-14). What is unusual is that he did this within the framework of the passover celebration in order to accentuate the predictable outcome of his confrontation with the ruling classes. Also he modified substantially the rite of the passover while relating it at the same time to what he referred to as "my hour." (Some texts permit the inference that the relationship between the words of Jesus and subsequent events was perhaps confused by the disciples at the time and that they did not fully understand the gesture until after the passion.)

The Climax of the Process of Delocalization

If, as we said in the first chapter, the God of Israel is linked with the movement of history and was dissociating the cult from specific places, then Christ completed this process. In response to the words of the Samaritan woman, "Our fathers worshiped on this mountain, while you say that Jerusalem is the place where one ought to worship," Jesus says, "Neither . . . nor . . .": "*neither* on this mountain *nor* in Jerusalem" (John 4:20-21). In the place where the temple was reconstructed, Jesus declares that he is greater than the temple (Matt. 12:6), and moreover, that he *is* the temple (John 2:19-22).

Thus the cosmological concept of the temple is definitively surpassed. *No longer is the cosmos the sanctuary but rather a man*, and to him Jews and Gentiles have access by faith. Circumcision no longer is a ticket for entry (Exod. 2:11-22). Some Greeks came to Philip and expressed their desire to "see Jesus" (John 12:22). Later they would be able to see "the one whom they had pierced" (John 19:37) when he was "lifted up from the earth" (John

12:32). The new temple therefore was the glorious and resurrected body of Christ, "the more perfect tent, which is better than the one made by men's hands" (Heb. 9:12). And everyone who in any place prays "to our Lord Jesus Christ" (1 Cor. 1:2) has entered the temple. From "a place" or "some places," a "certain place" has been reached, culminating the process of the delocalization of God made possible by the definitive "reconstruction" of the temple (his Body), which is precisely the result of the resurrection of Jesus, for "in his body lives the fullness of divinity" (Col. 2:9).

The early Christians who initially worshiped in the temple in Jerusalem—as can be seen in Acts 2:46 and 3:1-11—eventually recognized that they were the "living stones" of the new temple (1 Pet. 2:5). It is possible that the reinterpretation by which the concept of the Christ-temple (an individual) was transferred to the community (a group) was motivated by the difficulties that the Jewish Christians experienced in attempting to continue their assemblies in the Jewish temple—especially after the dispersion that took place following the death of Stephen (Acts 8:4 and 11:19)—and by the separation from Israel that resulted from the preaching to the Gentiles and the destruction of the temple A.D. 70. In 1 Corinthians 3:10-17, Paul refers to the idea of the construction and the destruction of a building. It is possible that the fire that he mentions is an allusion to the burning and razing of the temple in Jerusalem by Titus.[15]

Regardless of the basis of the Apostle's metaphor, Christians came to be regarded in his mind as temples of the Holy Spirit (1 Cor. 6:19) and "sanctuaries of God" in contrast with the idolatrous pagan temples. Thereafter, idols as things in the sanctuaries could not be regarded as significant as the "idols" that "lived" in the temple-persons. Today we refer to idols as internalized or subjectivized.[16]

Conflict with the Judaizers

The first Christians were Jewish Christians, and they were quite familiar with the traditional ideas and customs of the Jews. For this reason they observed certain customs: they respected the Levitical laws of purity (Acts 10:14), they observed the Jewish hours of prayer (Acts 10:9), and they went to the temple every day

(Acts 2:46; 3:1; 5:12, 20, 42). Luke records that the response to the ministry of Paul was affirmative when the elders of the Jerusalem church declared that there were thousands of Jews who had become believers, and "all of them staunch upholders of the Law" (Acts 21:20).[17] Moreover, it was suggested that in order to prove his fidelity to the Jewish law, Paul should associate himself with four of the Jewish Christians who apparently had taken a Nazarite vow, with the approval of James, the head of the church in Jerusalem(Acts 21:23-24).

A new ecclesial situation was necessary in order to liberate the gospel from its initial "identification" with the Jewish culture: persecution, preaching to the Gentiles, and contact with other cultures.

Initially Paul and Barnabas directed themselves to the Jews, among whom they were able to win some converts (Acts 13:1-43), but it was also Paul and Barnabas who encountered strong resistance from the Jews when as missionaries they attempted to carry the gospel to the Gentiles (Acts 13:50). The Jews were divided over the issue, and some even allied themselves with Gentiles in order to expel Paul and Barnabas from the city of Iconium (Acts 14:1-2).

The division among the Jews is clearly delineated in Acts 15:1-2—namely, that there were those who had insisted from the beginning that "the pagans should be circumcised and instructed to keep the Law of Moses" (Acts 15:5), while Paul and Barnabas held to the contrary. The question incited such controversy in the primitive Christian community that it became necessary to bring the issue before the Jerusalem church. Peter settled the question by affirming that "it would only provoke God's anger now, surely, if you impose on the disciples the very burden that neither we nor our ancestors were strong enough to support" (Acts 15:10). James supported Peter in adding that it would be wrong to impose upon the Gentiles unnecessary restrictions and conditions, but given the situation, he said: "I rule, then, that instead of making things more difficult for pagans who turn to God, we send them a letter telling them merely to abstain from anything polluted by idols, from fornication, from the meat of strangled animals, and from blood" (Acts 15:20). The final decision was communicated in writing through a special commission that accompanied Paul and Barnabas to Antioch in order that the letter from the Jerusalem conference be read and explained (Acts 15:22–29).

The struggle intensified, however, and soon Paul detected more and more resistance among the Jews. Finally he decided to desist altogether from preaching the gospel to the Israelites, and he set his face definitively toward the Gentiles (Acts 18:6). A study of Galatians 2 would seem to indicate that the Judaizers continued to harass the Apostle, following him and infiltrating the new Christian communities in order to foment opposition to his doctrine. Consequently, Paul had to warn these new believers repeatedly against the doctrines of the Judaizers, as can be seen by his contemptous reference to the "circumcisers" in Philippians 3:1–3. Also Paul states that on one occasion, at least, he felt obliged to confront Peter openly:

When Cephas came to Antioch . . . I opposed him to his face, since he was manifestly in the wrong. His custom had been to eat with the pagans, but after certain friends of James arrived he stopped doing this and kept away from them altogether for fear of the group that insisted on circumcision. . . . When I saw that they were not respecting the true meaning of the good news, I said to Cephas in front of everyone, "In spite of being a Jew, you live like the pagans and not like the Jews, so you have no right to make the pagans copy Jewish ways" [Gal. 2:11–14].

The good news was, according to Paul, that a person is not made righteous by obedience to the law but through faith in Jesus Christ (Gal. 2:16), for "if the law can justify us, there is no point in the death of Christ" (Gal. 2:21). It was also the Apostle's contention that—and he warned the Gentile Christians of this continually—to submit to the ritual of Levitical laws such as circumcision was to submit oneself "to the yoke of slavery" (Gal. 5:1–3). One can sense the virulence in Paul's caustic and satiric criticism when he says of circumcisers, "Tell those who are disturbing you I would like to see the knife slip" (Gal. 5:12)—that is, he wishes that they would go on and complete the job by castrating themselves.

When Paul went to Jerusalem (Acts 21)—well aware of the

danger that awaited him, and seeking to abide by the suggestions made to him by James—he was soon surrounded by a mob of Jews who "stirred up the crowd and seized him, shouting, 'Men of Israel, help! This is the man who preaches to everyone everywhere against our people, against the law, and against this place' " (Acts 21:28). People came running from everywhere, and Paul was dragged out of the temple and would likely have been killed if the Roman tribune and the cohort had not rescued him. The following day the Jews held a secret meeting and conspired to assassinate the Apostle (Acts 23:12-15). Though his enemies did not succeed in their plot, it is important to recognize that Paul was considered an enemy of the people, of the law, and of the temple, and he would have been eliminated had it not been for the protection afforded him by his Roman citizenship. One can see, therefore, the socio-religious characteristics of the conflict and the intensity of the hatred for him on the part of the Jews.

> The primitive church, at a given moment, found itself at a crossroads. If, listening to the adversaries whom Paul encountered at Antioch, in Galatia, at Corinth, and, without doubt, elsewhere and whose center of inspiration seemed to be at Jerusalem, it had imposed circumcision and the Law of Moses on the Gentiles, it would have stopped its recruitment and would have condemned itself to being nothing but a sect of Judaism believing in the Messiah, Jesus.[18]

It is evident that Paul is critical of the survival of the Jewish rites in Christianity under the impact of a new situation and succeeds in cutting Christianity free from the "umbilical cord" to which it is tied to the "mother church" and by means of it to Judaism. *It is Paul, therefore, who audaciously unfolds the universalist traits implicit in Christianity and who intuits the ultimate consequences of the discontinuity of Christianity with Judaism.* The Jewish womb was completely abandoned and Christianity liberated from its connection to Judaism. Christianity thus obtained characteristics that would be the basis for its further development.

The Christian abandonment of the Jewish rites resulted from: (1) the impact of the new historical situation, (2) the conflict that was no more than the difference in attitudes regarding the new situation, and (3) the struggle of Christianity with Judaism as well as the intraecclesial struggle among Christians themselves.

One also encounters here the fact that the primitive Christians—as the patriarchs of Israel earlier utilized the Canaanite sanctuaries (see Chap. 1)—utilized at first sanctuaries and synagogues of the Jews (Jesus himself taught in them) and their same rites, even though as Christians they had already recognized Jesus as the Messiah. Soon the new experience began to dislodge the "gods" that were there and to spell out the impossibility of any peaceful coexistence with them.

The unprejudiced historian finds in this historical moment the consciousness that their God (in this case Jesus Christ) was different, an awareness that obligated them to differentiate and characterize themselves as a group, and not the reverse. It is not the group already formed that characterizes its God, but a historico-religious experience of a different God that provokes the distinct characterization. They do not "project" the image of a different God because the group is different, but rather they become different *because* they perceive a different God. It is their experience with Jesus Christ that incites the conflict and little by little obliges them to distinguish themselves from Israel. We will see in the following discussion that this "suprastructural" datum influences the "infrastructure" of the primitive community, forming it into a *koinonia*.

The *Koinonia* of the Primitive Community

It is an incontrovertible fact that the primitive Christian community organized itself in a new way of living in the world, and in this sense attempted to reorganize history in conformity with its faith.

The suffering of their Lord produced a profound commotion in the apostolic community, in the people, and in their structures.[19] The breaking of the bread appears to be related to the owning of "everything in common" (*koinonia*) and to "the prayers." "The faithful all lived together and owned everything in common; they sold their goods and possessions and shared out the proceeds among themselves according to what each one needed" (Acts 2:44-45; 4:32, 35).

The situation in the church in Corinth illustrates this point. The Apostle Paul is extremely concerned because of the division that exists within the congregation (1 Cor. 1:10-11) and insists that these factions have divided the Body of Christ. He therefore asks, "Has Christ been parceled out?" (1 Cor. 1:13).

He then proceeds to censure the divisions that were evident in the assembly of the Corinthian Christian community and said, "When you hold these meetings, it is not the Lord's Supper that you are eating, because when the time comes to eat, everyone is in such a hurry to start their own supper that one person goes hungry while another is getting drunk" (1 Cor. 11:20-21). It was obviously the rich who were able to bring their own food, and they were sharing among themselves but not sharing with the poor. The well-to-do were insensitively gorging themselves and getting drunk while the poor went hungry. Paul violently condemns this kind of behavior, insisting that it was a disgrace to the church—the ecclesial Body of Christ—and likewise was embarrassing the poor, who did not have their own food and therefore were unable to participate (1 Cor. 11:22).

The Apostle then instructs the church that "every time you eat this bread and drink this cup, you are proclaiming his death so anyone who eats this bread or drinks the cup of the Lord unworthily will be behaving unworthily toward the body and the blood of the Lord" (1 Cor. 11:26-27), because these who "eat and drink without recognizing the body are eating and drinking their own condemnation" (11:29). Paul adds that when they are going to eat the memorial meal together, they must "wait for one another," and if any "are hungry," they "should eat at home," and then the meeting "will not bring your condemnation" (11:33, 34).

Current exegesis has established a distinction between the discernment of the resurrected body of Christ and the discernment of the ecclesial body.[20] For Paul these two perspectives not only intertwine, they are a single fact. They who do not practice the *koinonia* of their food or the *koinonia* of the bread, which is one and the same, do not discern that all of us are a single body, *because* we share a single loaf and we divide it, for the bread that we break is a communion with the body of Christ. "The fact that there is only one loaf means that, though there are many of us, we form a single body because we all have a share in this one loaf" (1 Cor. 10:17).[21] They who do not share the bread do not discern that "we many are one single body"—that is, they do not discern the ecclesial body of Christ. They despise the church (1 Cor. 11:22) and divide Christ (1 Cor. 1:13). Paul does *not* deny that the supper in Corinth is the supper of the Lord simply because they cannot distinguish between a common and a sacred meal (as most exegetes conclude). Rather he rejects their practice as a memorial of the Lord's death *because* they proceed to eat their own food and refuse to share their bread with the poor. For this reason he commands them to wait for one another *so that* their meeting will not bring their own condemnation (1 Cor. 11:34).

Schematically we can establish the following equation: To bring their own condemnation = not to wait for each other = for all to eat their own food = not to discern the body. The reverse is: To come together for health = to wait for one another = to eat the supper together = to discern the body.

The unavoidable conclusion is that if the bread is not shared, the supper of the Lord is not celebrated. And if the supper of the Lord is not celebrated, the fundamental proclamation that the church is to make before the world, the proclamation of the death of Christ, is not made.[22] The sin against the body of Christ is a sin against the ecclesial body of Christ, and not discerning the one is to fail to discern the other. We share the bread not because we are one body, but we are one body because we share the bread.

When the statement is made, "This is the body of the Lord," it is not merely the bread that is presented before the world as the body of Christ. It is also and primarily the community that shares or divides the bread that is presented as the body of the Lord. Only a church then that shares the bread proclaims the death of the Lord to the world. A church that refuses to share the bread is—rather than the body of the Lord—a "den of thieves." It nullifies, therefore, its verbal witness by its actions.

The division that Paul condemns is not a dogmatic, spiritual, or mystical division, but rather a social division. Nor is the *koinonia* of the primitive community—which Paul promotes

—a dogmatic, spiritual, or mystical unity (of hearts, as many say). It is the *koinonia* of *bread* and of *possessions*. It is an infra- and supra-structural *koinonia*.

The First Centuries of the Church

In the final years of the first century (or perhaps the beginning of the second), the *Didache* instructs Christians with regard to the Eucharist:

> And let no one who has a quarrel with a friend join you until they are reconciled lest your "sacrifice" be profaned.[23]

In the celebration of the eucharistic sacrifice, the necessity of unity among believers is especially stressed:

> Just as this loaf was previously scattered on the mountains,
> and when it was gathered together it became a unity,
> So may your church be gathered from the ends of the earth
> into your kingdom.[24]

St. Justin affirmed that the celebration of the Eucharist was the moment when Christians brought offerings, each one as they could, in order to help the "orphans and widows, and those who are in want on account of sickness or any other cause, and those who are in bonds, and the strangers who are sojourners among [us], and, briefly, . . . all those in need."[25] The Eucharist was, therefore, more than an act of devotion and piety; it was also a social act in which Christians shared their possessions with those in need. Eventually *this sharing was considered not something more or less secondary but an integral and indispensable part of the celebration.*

St. Cyprian castigated the rich because of their blindness to "the needy and the poor," and he went so far as to declare that if the rich came to the Mass without an offering for the poor, they could not participate in the sacrifice. "Do you rich and wealthy think that you celebrate the Lord's feast, you who do not at all consider the offering, who come to the Lord's feast without a sacrifice, who take part in the sacrifice that the poor person has offered?"[26]

The Church Fathers, however, did not treat the question of offerings for the poor as an issue in itself. They dealt with something far more basic and demanding, for they insisted that Christians not only share their goods with their neighbor, but also that the bishop in a city was a "watchman" among the people and was to be vigilant and make certain that the offerings were brought to the Mass for the community.[27] Furthermore, the Church Fathers insisted that a bishop receive no offering from those who oppress the weak.[28] "Those that oppress the widow and overbear the orphan, and fill prisons with the innocent, and abuse their own servants wickedly, I mean with stripes and hunger and hard service, nay, destroy whole cities; do thou, O bishop, avoid such as these and their odious oblations."[29]

The *Didascalia Apostolorum* insisted that in those cases when the churches were so destitute that there was no other means for feeding the hungry except by taking the money of the rich who commit injustices, it would be preferable to die of hunger than to accept anything from evildoers (*praestat vos fame perire quam accipere ab improbis*). The injunction was not an isolated one. It was given repeatedly at diverse times and in diverse churches:

> God saith to you: "To this end did you receive the gifts of the Levites, the first fruits and offerings of your people, that you might be sustained and even have over and above, that you might not be constrained to receive from evil persons." But if the churches are so poor that those in want must be supported by such, it were better for you rather to be wasted with famine than to receive from evil.[30]

The church maintained in those times the firm conviction that the Eucharist could not be celebrated while injustice and oppression were tolerated. On one occasion St. Ambrose, bishop of Milan, was informed that Emperor Theodosius had committed a brutal atrocity in the city of Thessalonica: he had summarily ordered the execution of several thousand persons. In response, Ambrose did not limit his repudiation of the emperor to a "prophetic denunciation." Rather the holy bishop's decision was precise and to the point. He wrote a letter to Theodosius in which he stated his reasons for refusing to meet him upon his return to Milan, and then he proceeded to censure him for the "atrocious" massacre at Thessalonica. The epistle concluded with an exhortation to Theodosius to repent. Ambrose declares, "I dare not offer the sacrifice if you intend to be present. Is that which is not allowed after shedding the blood of one innocent person allowed after shedding the blood of many? I do not think so."[31] There is no scarcity of sermons or documents protesting the suffering of the weak and the poor, but it should be perfectly clear that the Eucharist could not be compromised with political connivances or with violation and outrages, or high-handed, overbearing behavior of those who had responsibility in the empire and the provinces. The emperor had to admit and confess his sin and modify his conduct.

St. Basil, in the East, had done the same thing in rejecting the offering of an unjust prefect: "The emperor himself may hear this—that neither by violence nor persuasion will you bring us to make common cause with impiety, not even though your threats become still more terrible."[32]

The Eucharist, according to the vibrant expression of St. Irenaeus, was the "mark of liberty," the "offering . . . not by slaves, but by the free,"[33] so much so that, according to the greatest of the Church Fathers of the second century, this characteristic of freedom was the sign that distinguished the Christian Eucharist from all other types of religious celebration.

From the First Centuries to Vatican II

We will not attempt to follow step by step the liturgical itinerary of the church from the apostolic era until Medellín. What we will attempt is to indicate certain milestones in order to establish the relationship of the Eucharist to history.

The Lupercalia Festival

The Lupercalia was an ancient Roman fertility festival celebrated during mid-February. The celebration had, therefore, not only a folkloric meaning, but also a religious one: the magical rites were intended to assure the fertility not only of the people, but also of the animals and the fields. During the era of Pope Gelasius (492–496), the Lupercalia had assumed an almost total religious significance, becoming a kind of religious carnival. The pope, however, was disturbed by the notorious vices of paganism associated with the festival, and above all with the overshadowing moral dangers and the occasion for great abuses and scandals. Thus he began to struggle—using all his power and authority—to persuade the Christians of Rome to renounce participation in those orgies because of their incompatibility with the demands of the Christian faith.

We are today aware of the dimensions of this ardent campaign carried on by the pope through his famous letter *Adversus Adromachem contra Lupercalia.* Although addressed to the Roman Senator Andromachus, who together with other superstitious citizens was attempting to reinstitute the Lupercalia, it was meant for all the Christians of Rome who wanted to revive the pagan rite. What is important about the epistle is that Gelasius was not satisfied to limit the struggle to the question of a single festival, but he *obliged the Christian community to face the wider implications of the issue and thus carried the problem to the very heart of the liturgical celebration.*

This liturgical issue is evident also in the so-called *Leonine Sacramentary* or the *Sacramentarium Veronese*, which employed expressions so strong and penetrating in relating this problem to the liturgical celebration that some commentators have thought that these texts could never have been used by a pope in a normal public celebration of the Eucharist. Today, however, it has been proven that these formulas were composed by Pope Gelasius and were utilized in a completely orthodox celebration of the Eucharist in which the total Christian community participated, and that apparently no member of the eucharistic community was scandalized.[34]

This case clearly indicates how Pope Gelasius made the Eucharist an echo of the problems that were affecting his people, and at the same time he implored the community not only to reflect on the issue, but also to evaluate the repercussions of their participation in the event.

The Siege of Rome (537–538)

From April 23, 537, until March 4, 538, Rome was under siege by the Gothic armies of Vitiges. On March 29, 537, Vigilius was consecrated bishop of Rome and presided thereafter over the destinies of the church. The *Leonine Sacramentary* contains a large number of liturgical texts that Pope Vigilius composed during this time. It is evident that the liturgy incarnated a historical event, in this case a war. One can even follow the chronology of the famous siege carried on by Vitiges, even to the smallest details, by studying closely the liturgical texts utilized in the Christian celebrations of the Roman community. Moreover, the liturgy became the most important source for the historian in regard to certain points that otherwise would be obscure, particularly the determination of certain dates that are clearly evidenced from a detailed examination of the liturgical texts prepared by the pope for the Sunday Eucharist.[35] A liturgy that reflects the times to the extent that it becomes *a very important aid to historical research* demonstrates once again that liturgy cannot float above history without running the risk of becoming alienated.

A Language for the Liturgy

The reader may be surprised to learn that in all the history of liturgy there have been only two great revolutions in regard to the language used in the Mass.

Between the years 360 and 380 there was a transition from a liturgy in the Greek language to the liturgy in Latin. It is interesting to note that almost a century had passed since the Roman community had abandoned the use of Greek before the church decided to make a transition to Latin. Furthermore, it is important to note that this change was not made by a mere translation, but rather the Christian community of that time decided to create new texts that would express accurately and vividly the life and the deep feelings of the historical situation.[36] Thus from the fourth until the twentieth century—that is, until Vatican Council II—the Roman church in the West used only Latin in the liturgy, even though in the sixteenth century Protestants began to use the vernacular in their services of worship.

It was not until the Middle Ages, however, that the idea prevailed that the text used in the Roman Catholic services of worship was a text *reserved for the exclusive use in liturgy by the sacerdotal hierarchy.* This ceremonial restriction, therefore, tended to limit not only the translation, but also the diffusion of the liturgy and its study. In this regard a letter from Paris de Grassi written March 11, 1516, to Pope Leo X is very revealing:

> I respond above all to those who think that religious ceremonies should be made accessible to the majority of mortals. Your Holiness knows very well that the authority and the prestige of the Holy See depend on the dispositions that princes and the powerful maintain with respect to it. In effect, they believe that the pontiffs are not mortal men, but a species of gods on the earth; they submit to them, obey them, venerate, and almost adore them; they are captivated by an admiration without limits when they contemplate the ceremonies of canonization, of imperial coronation, of the anointing of kings, of the creation of cardinals, of the consecration of the patriarchs, archbishops, and bishops, or whatever other ceremony appears to include some divine feature. But if the secrets of worship are revealed and the ceremonies are made accessible, there will result immediately a loss of prestige.[37]

There is no need to comment on Grassi's assessment—only to note that it is impossible to express in a more disdainfully cynical way that worship had been converted into an esoteric and magical ceremony destined to assure the maintenance of power by the hierarchy.

In this same context one should note that the translation of the Roman Missal by Joseph de Voisin (1660) was placed on the *Index*, and that Alexander VII's Papal Brief *Ad aures nostras* of January 12, 1661, explicitly forbade the translation of the Missal even for private reading by the faithful. Clement IX's Papal Bull *Unigenitus* of September 8, 1713, rejected Proposition 86 of the Jansenist theologian Quesnel (who affirmed that "to remove from the simple people the consolation of uniting their hearts in prayer with all of the church is contrary to the apostolic practice and to the purposes of God"). On August 18, 1794, Pius VI in

Article 55 of the Synod of Pistoia declared that "the custom of employing the vernacular in liturgical prayers was false, rash, and to be prohibited."[38]

The Polemic of the Reformation

According to Max Thurian:

The Reformation took place at a period when an ultra-sacrificial theology of the Mass was to the fore. In this situation a reaction was inevitable; the simple Lord's Supper, as it was first celebrated, was rediscovered. But we must seek to understand further the reaction against the idea of sacrifice at the time of the Reformation, and in order to set this study within its context, it must be emphasized that the somewhat variable basis of this reaction was both biblical and pastoral. The Reformers discovered afresh in the gospels and in the writings of St. Paul that the Eucharist was first of all a *meal* and that it was therefore necessary to lay emphasis upon communion, as much from a dogmatic as from a pastoral point of view. But they were faced with a liturgical *practice* that emphasized above all the sacrificial and priestly aspect of the Mass, while the communion of the people was regarded as entirely secondary. To be present at Mass, as if at a sacrifice offered by a mediating priest, was alone obligatory. It was possible to be a good Catholic and to communicate only once a year at Easter. In the light of this, one can understand Luther's insistence on the real presence of the body and blood of Christ, not in relation to a repetition of the sacrifice of the cross, but in relation to the act of communion, which is an essential comfort for the people of God. Calvin himself laid the same emphasis upon the act of communion, although in his thought the doctrine of the real presence received a different expression.

The Eucharist is a communion; it is a meal in which one partakes; and it is not a sacrifice at which one is present or even in which one participates.[39]

In the apologetic environment of the Counter-Reformation, polemic post-Tridentine theologians elaborated all kinds of immolation "theories" (theologians such as Cajetan, Ruard Tapper, Melchior Cano, Salmerón, Suárez, and Bellarmine). Those theories of immolation and sacrifice soon became the common view in theological faculties—namely, that the Mass was a sacrifice. This prevailing notion proceeded to influence not only theology, but also popular preaching. Regarding these theories Father Chenu has said, "I was brought up with the old anti-Protestant and sanguinary theories."[40]

In light of the Catholic tendency to convert the Mass into *another* sacrifice, more or less autonomous and independent of the sacrifice on the cross, Protestants have insisted on the supper as a memorial of the suffering of Christ with the attendant danger of reducing it to a mere sentimental remembrance—a phenomenon that inspires Catholics to redouble their insistence on the "real presence."

From the period of the Counter-Reformation until our own day we find symptomatic verbalizations: "species," "appearances," "substance," "accidents," and finally "transubstantiation." *The total language of a structural sign*—the gestures that belong with the things, and the words that explain them—*were cut off and there occurred a reduction of the horizon of the total language of the Eucharist to a single language of things*. It was attempted to transfer to the thing the responsibility for saying what the ecclesial community was supposed to say—that is, "This is the body of the Lord."

It was not, therefore, the community with the total language of words and acts (structural signs) that should proclaim the death of Christ (*res*), but rather only the bread-thing and the wine-thing that should proclaim ("sign") the "real presence" of Christ (*res*). Even worse, nobody recognized that the bread-thing or the wine-thing was not merely a raw material, but rather was "the fruit of human labor," which says (or signifies) something absolutely different. The presence of Christ "placed" by the Bible primarily in the community (a historico-personal, anthropological concept) became primarily a thing generated as the result of a cosmological concept of the presence of Christ, which involved the accompanying dangers of misrepresentation, of magic, and of ritualism, and consequently of dehistoricalization. It is not a thing or the world, but the human being, the person, that is the primordial sacrament of Christ.

From a primarily anthropological, historical, and structural concept of sign, the bread and the wine came to be understood primarily as cosmological, ahistorical, and unstructural. The eucharistic language was ceremonialized and at the same time depersonalized. The church believed that mere "species" were sufficient for declaring the presence of Christ and relegated to a secondary plane the quality of Christ as a "sign lifted up among the nations," thus enervating the proclamatory *kerygma* of the Eucharist. The same can be said of the theories of "transsignification" and of "trans-finalization"[41] against whose dangers the encyclical *Mysterium Fidei* warned, dangers trapped in the barren environment of this cosmological reduction that does not recognize the most elemental principles of total language and of structuralism.

Within the context of this cosmological overevaluation of the "species" there remain such "problems" as the "separation of the species," which supposedly signifies the separation of the body and the blood of Christ,[42] but to our way of thinking typifies only the injection of the mentality of exegetes into the text. What is here injected and latently remains is the Greek concept that death results from the separation of the body (*soma*) and the soul (*psyche*). It is reasonably certain that the Hebrews considered the blood as the soul of the flesh (Gen. 9:1; Lev. 17:11; Deut. 12:23), and the "soul" to which reference is made in the Old Testament is the *nefesh* (life) and not the Greek *psyche*; the flesh of which they speak is the *basar,* or the Greek *sarx,* not the Greek *soma*, a word for which there is no equivalent in Hebrew.[43] Christ, therefore, could not have meant *soma* when he said, "This is my body," and the Hebrew *basar* and Aramaic *bisri* have been incorrectly translated as *soma*. In the Johannine Prologue, the "Word was made *sarx* (*basar*)," not *soma* (John 1:14), and it is this *sarx* that will be given, according to Jesus' reference in the last supper.

On the other hand, when Jesus refers to the blood that is to be shed, which, we repeat, for the Hebrews was the life (*nefesh*) of the flesh (*basar*), the disciples understood that there would be a shedding of blood and that Jesus was to be put to death. But what Jesus did was to continue with the wine-gesture the prophecy that began with the bread-gesture referring to his body, which was going to be given first (in time), and subsequently (in time) would be put to death by shedding his blood, the life (*nefesh*) of his flesh (*basar*). *Jesus refers, therefore, to two moments in the process and not to two constituent elements of his human nature.* These are two complementary moments of his suffering, two phases of the event that conforms to the historical truth of his suffering: he gave himself first, and later was put to death.

When the death of Jesus that is proclaimed in the Eucharist is made to reside completely in the separation of two things (bread-wine, body-soul), then the socio-political content is obscured, and what should be proclaimed is transferred to the thing that should be signified by the gesture: the breaking and the giving in the case of Christ, sharing and giving itself in the case of the ecclesial community. For the disciples of Jesus, what he said and what they understood was not so much the bread-thing or the wine-thing, but rather the gestures that Jesus made with them and that he explained with his words (remember that a different gesture with the same thing can signify something entirely distinct). Language in its entirety consists in the particular gestures a person makes with a thing (or several things) explained or disclosed by concomitant, accompanying words. The words in turn are verified or discredited by the facts or actions.

Vatican Council II

When one rereads the Constitution on the Sacred Liturgy of Vatican Council II (January 1964) and the Instruction for the Proper Implementation of the Constitution on the Sacred Liturgy (September 1964), one does not sense the joy of the conviction that here is an example of an audaciously progressive step forward. Rather the language suggests apprehensiveness, uncertainty, and almost resignation. Consequently, the "ifs," "ands," and "buts" seem to multiply. Is this understandable? Yes, because of the delicacy of the subject and certain historical hindrances. Even so, it is less than stimulating.

How should one understand, for example, those high prelates who affirmed that "though existing special exemptions are to remain in force, the use of the Latin language is to be preserved in the Latin rites" and the mother tongue is allowed in "certain circumstances" because it is "frequently a great advantage to the people"?[44] The obvious attitude of the prelates toward the people cannot be hidden, for the Constitution makes clear that they regard the "mother tongue" as "vulgar."

Nor can one ignore the fact that the council here adopts a condescending, princely air of concession. Apparently the prelates are not even aware of the fact that the language of the people is not merely of "great advantage" to them, but that it is always necessary and not only on special occasions. Why? Because faith, Paul tells us, enters by hearing and not by gibberish; and gibberish, as far as is known, is not understood by anyone (1 Cor. 14:9–11). The liturgy is a "parable in action." It is evangelization with gestures, with language, and not with gibberish. It is a sign and not only content. Why? Because language is not merely the sum of verbal formations or words. It is an expression of the mentality of a people. Liturgy therefore should be incarnated as an unequivocal expression of respect for the "genius and talents of the various races and nations" as the Constitution itself declares (No. 37).

We are not dealing here with something casual or unimportant. The Counter-Reformation church has insisted so much on the content (*res*) that it has obscured the sign (*signum*). Moreover, the sign that should be for the believer an open window to the content is obscured by rubrical flourishes and fog that block the access of the faithful to the faith. At the same time the rites are surrounded with a certain aura of intrigue and "mystery" (in the pejorative sense)—even to a kind of esotericism that redounds in prestige (ambiguous to be sure) to the clergy. We recall the words of Paris de Grassi cited above: "But if the secrets of worship are revealed and the ceremonies made accessible, from that moment there will be an immediate loss of prestige."[45] If the clergy desires to hold its position and prestige, then it will have to hold the people in ignorance. It appears, therefore, that the insistence on the content (*res*) cannot be sufficiently explained without determining the ideology of the class it represents. Correspondingly, insistence on the sign (*signum*) appears to correspond to the needs of the other class, but this deserves a more detailed study.

For this reason it is very encouraging to note that the council later declared: "The purpose of the sacrament is to sanctify persons, to build up the body of Christ, and finally to give worship to

God; *because they are signs, they also instruct*. They not only presuppose faith, but by words and objects they also nourish, strengthen, and express it."[46] It would have been more heartening had the Constitution declared that the sacraments have an evangelical purpose, but expectations are raised by what is said.

Although respect for the musical traditions of peoples in various parts of the world could have been anticipated,[47] the Constitution declares that "in the Latin church preference is to be given to the pipe organ" and to "Gregorian chant."[48] As to sacred art, the Constitution is explicit: "The church has not adopted any particular style of art as its own."[49]

The council fathers were obviously aware that if they were to admit the need for a liturgical reform they also had to provide the basis for such a reform. In this regard there are two very important references that deserve special mention because they indicate the awareness of churchmen that it was necessary "to make more responsive to the requirements of our own times those church observances open to adaptation"[50]—a position that we will subsequently call on to support with the same authority the suggestions that will be formulated in the third chapter of this work.

The Constitution declares: "For the liturgy is made up of *unchangeable elements* divinely instituted and of [other] *elements subject to change*. These not only may but ought to be changed with the passage of time if features have by chance crept in that are less harmonious with the intimate nature of the liturgy, or . . . have grown less functional."[51] Again: "Even in the liturgy, the church has no wish to impose a rigid uniformity in matters that do not involve the faith or the good of the whole community. Rather it respects and fosters the genius and talents of the various races and peoples."[52]

The liturgy, therefore, is flexible, changeable, and should reflect the pluralism of diverse situations in the world. That is, the liturgy should be incarnated. It should change with the *times* and should be a part of their *space*.

The liturgy is historical and geographical and subject to the same conditions as all valid change: continuity and discontinuity. Moreover, the desire that now surges in Christian circles to reform the liturgy is not a passing fancy or the superficial urge for novelty. It is the longing to incarnate the sign: "Zeal for the promotion and restoration of the liturgy is rightly held to be a sign of the providential dispositions of God in our time, as a movement of the Holy Spirit in his church. It is today a distinguishing mark of the church's life, indeed of the whole tenor of contemporary religious thought and action."[53]

Conclusions

1. Jesus explicated the definitive anthropocentric significance of religious cult, putting the cult of praxis and of justice above the formalistic cult of words, and emphasizing fellowship as the precondition of cult, thus placing in relief the human action that precedes and qualifies the offering.

2. Jesus celebrated with his disciples the feast of independence of his nation (the passover) in the context of the Jewish passover, the environment also of his suffering or pasch. He did not come to abolish . . . (continuity).

3. Jesus, however, introduced a fundamental variation in the celebration in that precisely by his insistence on its newness, he surprised his disciples that night. He came to give meaning . . . (discontinuity).

4. Basically this discontinuity consisted in connecting the passover with *his hour*, commanding his disciples to celebrate it in the future in memory of him.

5. This connection was realized by two prophetic gestures of warning that prefigured his self-giving and his death, and that also dramatized both of them.

6. One of these gestures was with the bread, which he broke and gave to them saying, "This is my body that is given (sign)." And with it he alluded to the historico-political event of his betrayal by Judas and condemnation by Caiaphas and Pilate, representing the Gentiles (*res*).

7. The other was with the wine that was poured and given by Jesus who said, "This is my blood that is shed (sign)," and with it he alluded to the historico-political event of his death, which was already in course (*res*).

8. The depoliticizing of the death of Jesus depoliticizes his resurrection. And the depoliticizing of both translates into a liturgical depoliticization. The reason for depoliticizing the death and

resurrection appears to be based on the supposition that the signs (*semeia*) of Jesus had a different content (*res*) from the events lived out by Jesus and his historico-political denouement, which was translated in the self-giving and in the betrayal and death of Jesus.

9. The Eucharist is not the proclamation of the death of a person who died by natural causes. It is rather the proclamation of a death that was entirely the result of an injustice, in which the sin of the world is concentrated. To proclaim with the Father the resurrection of Christ, we participate with God in revealing the "execution" as an injustice, thus unmasking the sin of the world, vindicating Christ, and thereby judging the world.

10. Returning Jesus to life, which the powerful of his time had taken from him, the Father "topples the powerful from their throne," annihilating the worst that they could do to quench the struggle for justice. The annihilation (negation) thus placed in the hands of all those who had been wronged the most powerful weapon to continue the struggle: the hope of resurrection. The resurrection is, therefore, the *ultimate basis for rebellion*. And for this same reason, "the negation of the resurrection of the dead is an ideology defensive of the status quo; it is the silencing of the sense of justice that history objectively stirs up; it is to kill the nerve of the real hope of changing this world."[54]

11. The temple was not a cosmological place but rather a person and a community. This (anthropologically) historifies the presence of God, which overcomes a purely cosmological presence.

12. The Christian liturgy withdrew from identification with Jewish culture under the impact of a new historical situation and by reason of a conflict that Christians had with Jews and among Christians themselves.

13. The characterization that the Christian community made of their God (Christ) prompted them to characterize themselves as a group. Their characterization of themselves, therefore, did not precede their characterization of their God. Their progressive separation from Israel, nevertheless, was the result of a conflict first with the Jews and later with the Greek and Roman cultures in which they developed their christologies.

14. This characterization affected the infrastructure of the primitive community, shaping the *koinonia* (of food and of their

other possessions), which had as its center of operations and expression the Eucharist.

15. According to Paul, those who did not share the bread did not discern that "though there are many of us, we form a single body because we all have a share in this one loaf." Those who do not discern this do not celebrate the supper of the Lord and are failing to make the fundamental proclamation that the church should make in the world.

16. During the early centuries the church demonstrated that the Eucharist was *koinonia* and that the *offerings* of those who oppress the poor—*qui pauperes opprimunt*—were not to be received, because such offerings were the fruits of injustice.

17. Subsequently, the church brought into the very heart of the Eucharist the historical problems that existed (the Lupercalia and the siege of Rome).

18. The problem with liturgical language is that it results from an exaggerated insistence on the *res* (the matter) and ignores the *signum* (the sign). Furthermore, it appears to have a relationship with the ideology of a clerical class thirsting for prestige.

19. Protestants reacted against the "bloody" ultra-sacrificial theories and insisted that the Eucharist was the supper. The question was not whether to attend a sacrifice or to participate in it. The question was communion in the supper. The issue centered not on another sacrifice but on the memorial of Christ's passion.

20. The discussion regarding the "real presence" of the bread-thing and the wine-thing overlooks the structural presence of Christ in the community-temple and returns to a view of the cosmological presence of divinity that reduces the total language of the Eucharist (structural sign).

21. The gesture with the bread and the wine does not refer to two constituent elements of the human nature of Christ (a Greek mentality) but to the two historical moments of his passion, the background of which was the climax of the conflict between the dominant classes and Jesus.

22. Finally, Vatican Council II timidly opened the question of the language that was called "vulgar" and rediscovered the pedagogical purpose of the liturgy. It also affirmed that the liturgy is an institution subject to change and therefore should be pluralistic. And the council affirmed that the desire to reform the liturgy constituted a sign of the Spirit.

CHAPTER THREE

Elements for the Design of a Eucharist (A Reinterpretive Essay)

The same celebration must be taken to the poor and the marginalized and produce in them a progressive awareness of their unity as a people and of the exigencies that follow from this awareness. From one Eucharist to another there should grow in them the pride and the responsibility of being human beings, so that their constant eucharistic participation will motivate them to raise their heads and move toward the encountering and procuring of a liberty that is not optional but is a right, and of which only they can be the legitimate authors.

—Archbishop Rubén Isaza, Third Letter to the Faithful of Cartagena

The Liturgy in the Documents of Medellín

Having already reviewed, in a brief way to be sure, the charge of hope in the Judeo-Christian tradition, we will now attempt to present not a design for the Eucharist for Latin America, but something much more modest. That is, we will suggest *certain elements* for such a design. We are aware that this is the most delicate part of our work, and that it would be much easier and less hazardous to bypass it. But as we indicated in the Introduction, we consider this section indispensable and for this reason have run the risk of including it.

This first point, which could have been the last point of the previous section, we have preferred to place here because our hope is to realign, harmonize, the liturgy with the aspirations of our continent.

In order to set forth its peculiarities, we turn again to the Constitution of Vatican Council II, which will demonstrate clearly the differences in perspective between it and Medellín.

The first evident difference is that in Medellín the liturgical text is Document 9. In the Second Vatican Council the Constitution on the Sacred Liturgy was the first work completed by the prelates. Pope Paul said that "the liturgy was the first subject to be examined and the first too, in a sense, in intrinsic worth and in importance for the life of the church." [1] In Medellín the liturgy occupied a more subordinate position, for there the primary attention was given to the questions of justice and peace (Documents 1 and 2).

This is not a minor difference, as will be evident in the succeeding discussion. We are aware that for Vatican II the liturgy is "the summit toward which the activity of the church is directed; at the same time it is the fountain from which all its power flows," [2] a concept that is ecclesiocentric and liturgicocentric.

For Medellín, "the liturgical celebration crowns *(cumbre)* and nourishes *(fuente)* a commitment to *the human situation,* to development and human promotion." [3] This implies a centrifugal ecclesiology on the one hand and an awareness of the unicity of history on the other, "precisely because all creation is grafted onto the saving design that includes all humankind." [4]

The liturgical concept of Vatican II is a dualistic perspective in which the church considers itself the collective subject of a sacred history parallel to secular history, or in the best of cases, as being closely united to secular history. But in Medellín the liturgy emerges as the climax of the efforts for development, promotion, and liberation of Latin America and entails a new commitment to these efforts. For Medellín the liturgy should be, so to say, a "stop along the way"[5] where we celebrate festively *our* history *and* its paschal, eschatological meaning. We are not suggesting here a parenthesis in our history in order to celebrate another history, but rather the recapturing and the reassuming of it by taking great pains to discover its profound meaning and accepting the challenges that that meaning implies in order to carry it to its final conclusion.

If "the progressive movement of the People of God toward their eschatological fulfillment [is] now expressed in the liturgy,"[6] then the liturgical sign should be expressive not only in measuring what has already been accomplished in moving toward this fulfillment (memorial) but also in measuring what is lacking in order to reach it (prophecy). It should memorialize, therefore, the Latin American achievements in which Christ has been actively present[7] *and* be a prognostic sign of the tasks that we should attempt in order to realize eschatological fulfillment. "God has raised Christ from the dead, and also therefore all those who believe in him. Christ, actively present in our history, foreshadows his eschatological action not only in the impatient zeal of humankind to reach total redemption, but also in the conquests that, like prophetic signs, are accomplished by human action inspired by love."[8] The Eucharist should be a memorial to inspire us to what we can do and a prophecy to challenge us to attempt what appears to be impossible. It should be a stimulus and a challenge, a cry of liberation and of hope. It should serve as "the passage for each and all, from conditions of life that are less human to those that are more human."[9]

Despite a long Catholic tradition that insisted, beginning in the sixteenth century, on the real presence, Vatican II was obliged to admit, and not without a certain resignation, that "the purpose of the sacraments is to sanctify persons, to build up the body of Christ, and finally, to give worship to God." But *"because they are signs, they also instruct.* They not only presuppose faith, but by words and objects they also nourish, strengthen, and express it."[10] Medellín in contrast placed the liturgy under the section entitled "Evangelization and Growth in the Faith," indicating that the Latin American bishops regarded it as concerned primarily with *kerygma,* or proclamation of the gospel.

There is something that stands out in a special way in the Me-

liturgy - celebration of a tension

dellín document on the liturgy: *its awareness of sin*. In contrast it is like "looking for a needle in a haystack" in the Constitution on the Liturgy of Vatican II to find any indication of an awareness of sin. In 130 paragraphs sin is referred to only once, and then in regard to the penitential elements of Lent. Regarding catechesis, the Constitution here declares, "It is important to impress on the minds of the faithful not only the social consequences of sin, but also the fact that the real essence of the virtue of penance is hatred for sin as an offense against God."[11]

For the bishops in Medellín, "all liturgical celebration is essentially characterized by the *tension* between what is already a reality and what has not yet fully come to pass. . . . It has a sense of joy and *a painful awareness of sin*."[12] "In Latin America this affirmation signifies that the liturgy should indicate clearly with a total language of words and signs the distance between the actual Latin American situation and the purpose and intent of God. Otherwise there is no celebration of a tension,"[13] and there is no awareness of sin, without which things will remain as they are.

One should not assume, however, that Medellín calls for a recognition of the presence of sin in order to enjoy it in some morbid fashion and then accept it as being merely an expression and reflection of the de facto culture. This would be the crudest form of positivism and the most cynical kind of complicity. The primary purpose is not to "present sin in society" but rather to expose sin for what it really is. The liturgy, it must be affirmed, "cannot be reduced to the mere expression of a human reality, frequently one-sided or characterized by sin, but must rather judge this reality, leading it to the fullness of Christian meaning."[14]

The Eucharist should, therefore, be a kind of prophetic crisis that calls into question the status quo in order to provoke a change in thinking and action. The purpose, we repeat, is not to give sin an opportunity for making a formal entrance into society, but rather to judge it and to unmask it. If we are ingenuously unaware of the accused or if we refuse to judge them, this is not prophecy and it quickly dissolves the tension that should be celebrated. It negates hope and remains caught in the trap of positivism.

"Positivism, we should remember, limits thinking to the given and confines action to the established order," as Roger Garaudy rightly observed.[15] And, what is worse, it defends what it has done even without desiring to do so, because to limit oneself solely to reflecting on or describing the de facto situation is to convert the situation into *a mechanism for propaganda and for duplication of the system.* This is even more dangerous when it is confirmed by the accolade of the sacred. It implies—without saying so—that the system is the will of God, and no honest person can confuse this *kerygma* with the gospel of Jesus Christ.

The Eucharist as a political sign does not depend on the will of the church (voluntarism). It will be a political sign in one way or another whether the church is aware of it or not. There is nothing more dangerous than an unrecognized power, because one who is political without knowing it is an easy victim of manipulation. But if the Eucharist is to be intentionally a political sign, the church will have to be aware of the relationship between faith and politics, the church itself being a case in point.[16]

That the Eucharist (and the liturgy) be an expression and reflection of the de facto situation is something *logical* and *necessary,* but it is *insufficient.* As such it is nothing more than descriptive and statistical sociology that never passes to the interpretative phase. If it does not become a judgment *(krisis),* it remains in the middle of the road straitened by the walls of positivism. That the Eucharist (and the liturgy) be adapted to and incarnated in the various cultures, including their folklore (a phase not fully attained even in Latin America), is absolutely necessary; but, we repeat, this is not *sufficient.* The Word became incarnate not merely to be with us but primarily and more importantly to provoke a crisis. Jesus declared, "It is for judgment that I have come into this world" (John 9:39).

Finally we should keep in mind that when the bishops at Medellín referred to sin, they did not have in mind only, or primarily, private sin, those individual and personal deviations from the Judeo-Christian norm—as some groups emphasize—but rather structural and social sin. Sin in this context is the situation of injustice that is called "institutionalized violence."[17] It is the whole situation that is sinful.[18] It is "poverty, as a lack of the goods of this world necessary to live worthily as human beings" that is "in itself evil."[19] The prophets denounced poverty, the bishops noted, "as contrary to the will of the Lord and most of the time as the fruit of human injustice and sin."[20] These are the causes of the tensions that conspire against peace. The oppression of the dominant sectors, the opposition of these sectors to any substantial change, the repression, the international colonialism, the sale and distribution of armaments, are all elements of this sinful situation. They represent not merely the sin of the church. They are manifestations of the sins of the world that emanate from every pore of society. As such they constitute the principal target of ecclesial action. Here is the sin that the Eucharist should unequivocally indict.

Camilo Torres and Priorities

Medellín was a first attempt by church leaders to give a global response to the questions that had been formulated in the Latin American mind. In this sense, however, it was more than the ecclesial expression of the maturing Latin American consciousness, which had begun to develop our own perception of our history, of our situation, and of our destiny. It was not by chance, therefore, that at the same moment that Latin America began to acquire its own personality, the attempt was made by the church and by Latin American theologians to spell out the implications of this consciousness. One may assert, therefore, that in a great number of cases, the absence of an authentic *ecclesial* Latin American awareness resulted simply from the lack of an authentic Latin American awareness.

There were many Christians who anticipated Medellín in this experience of the bourgeoning "Latin Americanness," but among them the one who stands out most dramatically is Father Camilo Torres Restrepo, who shook the whole continent with his prophetic deeds and words. For this reason he must be mentioned in this work.

What was most surprising was, without doubt, his decision to commit himself to politics, which necessarily demanded the abandonment of his specific functions as a pastoral priest. Note that we refer to the *pastoral* priesthood and not to the priesthood as such, which in no sense is the monopoly of a single ecclesial sector, but rather the property of all the people of God, as the New Testament clearly teaches. Also it is well known that the Catholic

Church has a structure that is strictly clerical, in which the division between the clergy and the laity is strongly and abusively accentuated, and which was denounced forcefully by Luther in the sixteenth century. To this division Camilo referred in his letter to Archbishop Rubén Isaza, labeling it "the cultural and sociological separation between the clergy and the faithful," and characterizing it as one of the social and psychological factors that must be eliminated if a conscious and personal adherence to the church to be fostered.[21] This division of classes, socio-religiously at least, but also as related to social classes from an economic point of view, has not been overcome by the Catholic Church, not even with a theology that explains that the laity *also* are the church!

Unfortunately in Colombia the Catholic Church and the people in general—because of the image that the clergy promotes—conceive of the pastoral ministry as absolutely clerical on the one hand and totally centralized in worship on the other. But the epochs of ministerial decadence, as Segundo Galilea points out, have always been characterized by this blunder, in Judaism as well as in Christianity. "A ministry enters or falls into decadence," he says, "when it is clericalized and centered in worship. And habitually, the criteria for judging the pastoral quality of a ministry remain closely tied to the roots of the clerical nature of this ministry and to the volume of the ritual functions."[22]

Thus the criticism by most of the clergy and the great majority of the Colombian people in judging the quality of the decision of Camilo was clearly clerical and ritualistic, whereas for him the priority was quite the opposite. "In my concept," he said, "the emphasis should be put on the means for establishing the kingdom, and should be in the following order: (1) Lead the people to love, with a love of self-giving *(agape)*. (2) Preach the gospel. (3) Public worship: the Eucharist and the sacraments (as also sacramentals and paraliturgical functions)."[23]

What was for the Colombian people primary (public worship) was for Camilo the least important. There was, therefore, no possibility of understanding and even less of agreement.

Only if we keep in mind the premises that we have established, the order set forth by Camilo, and the context of social injustice that he described *as a sociologist,* can we understand the appropriateness of his decision. "As a sociologist," he said, "I have desired to see this love become efficacious through technology and science. But upon analyzing Colombian society I have become aware of the necessity of a revolution in order to be able to give food to the hungry, drink to the thirsty, clothing to the naked, and to promote the well-being of the majority of the people of our country."[24] What we see here is the relationship established by Camilo between sociology and theology, which afterwards will have to be worked out by Latin American Christians.

These were the words with which Camilo explained his decision to the nation:

> When there exist circumstances that impede persons from coming to Christ, the priest has as his personal function and responsibility the combating of these circumstances, *even at the cost of the possibility of celebrating the eucharistic rite,* which cannot be understood without the involvement of Christians. . . .
>
> The Christian priesthood does not consist only in the celebration of external rites. The Mass, which is the final objective of the sacerdotal function, is fundamentally a community function. But the Christian community cannot offer the sacrifice in an authentic way if it has not fulfilled, in an effective degree, the precept of loving one's neighbor.[25]

He concluded by suggesting the possibility of returning to offer Mass and cited the words of the gospel: "So then, if you are bringing your offering to the altar and there remember that your brother has something against you, leave your offering there before the altar, go and be reconciled with your brother first, and then come back and present your offering" (Matt. 5:23–24).

Obviously Camilo did not abandon the priestly ministry in order to become reconciled with one individual—something that is usually done before the celebration of the Eucharist—but rather to struggle for the creation of the objective conditions that would make human fellowship possible; in his sociological analysis, they did not exist. Consequently with his priorities he considered that such a struggle was clearly Christian and priestly, and at the same time he exposed the real problem by denouncing the peaceful—and cynical—coexistence of the liturgy with a situation of sin and injustice.

At no time did Camilo imply that the celebration of the Eucharist should be suspended until the revolution was achieved or until justice was complete—which will only happen at the Parousia, when it will no longer be necessary to celebrate Mass. This interpretation has been attributed to him by tendentious minds, which have not made the slightest effort to understand his point of view, critics who have revealed their own ideologies by interpreting him in this way. The intuition of Camilo points to the imbalance (or contradiction) between the Eucharist as a sign and Colombian history as the content. This suggests, on his part, the intuition that the Eucharist cannot be a "floating sign" in our history, but is a "fixed" sign in our reality, not merely for reflection (positivism), but also and primarily for judging history (prophecy). As a prophetic clarion he raised his voice to show that worship was coexisting peacefully and cynically with injustice and sin.

The priests and pastors who, under the effect of a Platonic dualistic perspective, did not understand the interconnection between sacred rites and our everyday reality, logically remain puzzled not only by the fact that Camilo committed himself completely to politics in order to create the conditions possible for love (the supreme norm of Christianity, as he himself called it), but also because, according to them, he grossly underestimated ritual practices. But in reality they overvalued them and did not understand his connection with an articulation of real history.

The Eucharist as the School of Liberation[26]

The Liturgy of Liberation

Here our preoccupation is to indicate a possible way for relating the faith with the reality of our continent. This is the reason why we insist on the necessity of restructuring the Eucharist according to our situation of dependence—the theoretico-interpretive key to our reality in which "the language of liberation" is "nothing more than the political correlative of the socio-analytic language of dependence."[27]

Every liturgical meeting is a meeting of free persons who proclaim the paschal liberation of the Lord Jesus Christ in order to give testimony to the liberty of the children of God.

The word of God is the source that introduces us to the mystery of the paschal liberation of Christ; from it, as the Israelites did, we learn and we review the history of salvation. Here we receive the directions for our own liberation. For this reason, we always proclaim the word of God in every liturgical assembly, and thereby we are celebrating, promoting, and realizing the liberation of humanity.[28]

Today we should make it clear that what we ought to learn and ponder in the school of the Eucharist is our own history of salvation and, even more, our own history, given the salvific character of all history. We should at least appropriate from those heroic exploits that we have entered into paschally the energy to move from conditions of a life less human to something more human, stages that constitute milestones on our march toward ultimate fulfillment.

If the Jewish passover celebrated the liberation of the Jewish people, the Christian passover celebrates the liberation of all peoples. The Eucharist is the banquet of the liberty of the children of God. But also in the Jewish passover the people reviewed and renewed the commitment to the covenant that Yahweh made with them at Sinai. For this reason the Eucharist obliges us to review and renew the commitment we have made to Christ to collaborate with him in the total liberation of all human beings.[29]

Here we want to cite a lengthy passage from the pastoral letter of Rubén Isaza, archbishop of Cartagena, given its importance and its connection with our theme:

> When in the church we celebrate the Eucharist we proclaim the justice of the bread distributed to all equally, liberty for all who come together to celebrate the paschal mystery. In our passover, it should be said, our liberty, which is celebrated here, is, in terms of the kingdom, that which is prefigured and anticipated.
>
> I wonder if the Eucharist—at which I preside and which I celebrate with you—is authentic and sincere. I respond: *My doubts regarding the authenticity of this celebration begin when it is evident that ours is not a system of social life conformed to justice. . . .* Social conflicts are continually evident, imbalances and inequalities exist among us to such

a degree that it raises serious doubt as to the sincerity and the authenticity of the Eucharist that we celebrate.

When I see the needs, those resigned to their fate with a passive acceptance of life conditions that make impossible for them any access to human dignity or who are pressured into a state of awaiting government help and are not actively struggling to promote for themselves a life of greater dignity, I conclude that *the Eucharist celebrated by us cannot be a sign or a source of liberation or equality.*

It is not in passivity or in conformity that the Christian realizes communion with God. Rather it is in the attempt without respite to achieve one's own liberation, and by the continual movement forward from a life less human to conditions more human. It is clear that in this matter we Christians do not want to recognize our own culpability. But we will be culpable if we refuse to understand that, just as in the first passover of the Israelites, *the Eucharist ought to be received by those who are ready to begin the march toward their liberation.*

This craftsmanship of peace, this promotion of the love of Christ, *is required as a condition for a sincere eucharistic celebration* as long as conditions persist that drive many to extreme reactions out of desperation. The eucharistic celebration should therefore launch the poor and the marginalized toward a progressive awareness of their dignity as human beings and of the demands that arise from this fact. From Eucharist to Eucharist they should grow in their own self-esteem and in their acceptance of their own responsibility as human beings, *so that their continual eucharistic participation will motivate them to raise their heads in order to move toward the pursuit and the conquest of a liberty that is not an option but a responsibility and a right, and of which only they can be the legitimate authors.*[30]

As Archbishop Isaza contends, the Eucharist should be received by those who are ready to begin the march toward their own liberation. It should involve only persons who are disposed to be free from their sin, from their egotism, from their enslavements. We can declare, therefore, that, when we come together to hear the liberating word of the gospel and we receive the liberating bread of God, *this is the most aggressive gesture of nonconformity with the enslavements that oppress human beings.*[31]

This gesture of nonconformity will be authentic to the degree that it expresses a genuine historical aggressiveness against the varied forms of slavery. The fact is that the eucharistic act is not in itself protest, nonconformity, or aggressiveness.

The Eucharist as Protest

Segundo Galilea alludes to the "protest Masses" that were celebrated in Colombia, Bolivia, Chile, and in other countries of Latin America immediately following Medellín, and that, he says, pose the following question: "Do these protest Masses indicate that the other Masses and liturgies are conformist?" From his response we extract what appears to be the substance of his answer:

> I believe precisely the contrary. All authentic Eucharists, conscientiously celebrated, may be considered as acts of protest, of social protest in Latin America, of the most radical and absolute kind. The Eucharist is the explicit proclamation of the lordship of Christ, the unique Liberator and the only Lord of history and of humankind. Thus it is proclaimed not simply that Christ is the only Lord, but also that his lordship excludes all other dominions and lordships over humanity, and that in him we have become finally free. Socially speaking, it is proclaimed that we reject completely every kind of oppression that impedes human beings from achieving their destiny.
>
> This declaration conscienticizes us and can become a cause for radical social nonconformity when the participants in the Eucharist are persons who suffer any kind of domination. Socially speaking, *the Eucharist periodically celebrated should be a loud cry of alarm and of protest, disquieting and awakening us to socio-political responsibilities.* In this sense the religious action—and above all the eucharistic action—is extremely dangerous for every inhuman and oppressive system.

The leaven of nonconformity that pervades the Christian liturgy will not stop with socio-economic kinds of oppression alone. It will remove all the new idols that tend to imprison humanity.

The absolute liberty intrinsic in the proclamation of Christ as the only Savior is subversive vis-à-vis every totalitarian system.[32]

The informed reader will note that in regard to the question of whether the protest Masses make the other Masses and liturgies appear conformist, Galilea responds not by analyzing what they have become *in fact,* but by contrasting them to what all authentic Eucharists *should be.* In a sense this avoids the basic question and cushions the answer with an apologetic overtone. But the author's inadvertence does not lessen the importance of the substance of his response, to which we subscribe.

We should like to add one other notation. If we rely on the mere reading of the text (without prejudging Galilea's intentions, which are perhaps different) we are left with the impression that the author considers such liturgical efforts as nothing more than the fancies or deviations of rebel priests who are imprudent and undisciplined, and not as outlines—certainly imperfect, given their character of improvisation and of pastoral urgency—of the future Latin American liturgy we and many others have to consider.

Galilea's reflections appear to have been made *on the occasion of* (or because of) some protest Masses considered in themselves as liturgical deviations, but which call attention to a yet unnoticed aspect regarding the liturgy. His final words appear to corroborate our judgment:

> I am not attempting to justify the ill-named protest Masses, or to say that the Eucharist and the liturgy should be reduced to such Masses. What I want to say is that this aspect of the Eucharist should be made much more explicit because it is one of the messages that God today is giving to the Latin American people.[33]

We, in contrast, consider these Masses as constituting a legitimate *locus theologicus.* They constitute a prognostic sign of the kind of liturgy viable for Latin America, a liturgy that will challenge the responsible theologian to assume them as the beginning point for critical reflection. Obviously theology cannot be reduced to a task of justifying Christian experience, but neither is it simply a mechanism for defending things as they are. The real challenge for Latin American theology is to take as the content for critical reflection precisely the experiences of the Christians who are making the church on our continent, and even more concretely to reflect on their political praxis of liberation. We would affirm that the protest Masses are not deviations but rather challenging liturgical *correctives*. Their fundamental intuition points to the articulation of the liturgy with history in Latin America, emphasizing the liturgy as crisis (judgment) and challenging the creative imagination. In them we find the direction taken by Camilo Torres and recommended by Archbishop Isaza in the texts we have already cited.

We believe that the Eucharist can be "extremely dangerous for every inhuman and oppressive system" to the degree that it is supported by an "extremely dangerous praxis." We also believe that the proclamation of Christ can be dangerous for all totalitarian systems to the degree that the proclaimer profoundly identifies with the plan and purpose of the people. In reality the mere proclamation of the lordship of Christ does not change anything. But if the lordship of the people is proclaimed, then repression immediately follows.

The Eucharist: A Particular Example of Church-World Relations

If on the one hand the Eucharist is a condensed epistemological moment that the church recovers or recaptures in order to rethink and revise its mission in and with the world, and if on the other hand the gathered church is not supra-humanity, nor parallel-humanity, nor even anti-humanity, but humanity *reflexively* "christified,"[34] humanity distinguished by "a difference in the level of consciousness," then Latin Americans who celebrate the Eucharist are not—and this we must emphasize—themselves supra-Latin Americans, or parallel-Latin Americans, or even anti-Latin Americans, but simply Latin Americans. They are Latin Americans who, *conscious of the paschal rhythm of their history,* recover this history (and in this sense recover themselves) to celebrate its paschal and eschatological meaning, recovering anew in the process the purpose of their historical thrust. They imagine by and in this "parable in action" not only their history, but also the unexplored universe of their own potentials.

According to Harvey Cox, rites are to society what fantasy is to the individual.[35] Eucharist is therefore collective imagination that creatively fantasizes our history.

We would assert that if "the church does not signify the church but signifies humanity,"[36] then the relation of church to humanity is the same as that of sign to content. And the Latin American Eucharist, the "moment in which the church is most perfectly itself,"[37] is—or should be—to the history of Latin America what the sign is to the content. Visualize it in the following formula:

$$\text{If} \ldots \quad \frac{\text{Church}}{\text{World (or History)}} \; = \; \frac{\text{Sign}}{\text{Content}}$$

$$\text{Then} \ldots \quad \frac{\text{Latin American Eucharist}}{\text{Latin American History}} \; = \; \frac{\text{Sign}}{\text{Content}}$$

To put it even more clearly: *the content of the Latin American Eucharist is (or should be) the history of Latin America.*

It should memorialize, therefore, the Latin American liberation in which Christ has been actively present[38] and it should be a prognostic sign of the liberations that should be achieved in order to realize eschatological fulfillment.[39] Latin Americans, therefore, do not celebrate another history, but their *own* history, and they are not committed to another history but to their own history, just as Jesus himself celebrated his history and self-giving for the people.

It is possible that at this point readers are somewhat surprised or even scandalized, and that there is floating around in their minds questions such as the following: Have you not reduced the Eucharist to nothing more than a secular event or patriotic celebration? Have you not Latin-Americanized the Eucharist to the extent that you have emptied it of its sacred content? And have you not therefore disqualified it as a sacred sign? Where then are

Christ and his paschal mystery? Is this not a typical case of historical and secular reductionism? Even more, how can you even call this the Eucharist?

I will begin by repeating what I have said before. "All national history is also sacred history, and for that reason it is preparation for the coming of Christ. God speaks to us in all local histories."[40] The paschal mystery of Jesus Christ is not the private property of Israel or of the church. Rather it includes and affects the entire history of humanity and the eschatological meaning that this history has in itself and in all its parts.

Approximately one hundred fifty years ago we were able to free ourselves from Spanish domination, and we would say that we moved from "conditions of life that were less human to conditions of life that were more human."[41] In this way our country began its paschal mystery, much as Israel began its paschal mystery when it was liberated from Egyptian oppression. And given the fact that "all liberation is an anticipation of the complete redemption of Christ,"[42] that achievement of independence from a foreign power moved us effectively toward the kingdom of liberty. The past, nevertheless, should not divert us, and we cannot live merely by remembering a partial liberation. Today we are committed to the future.

The true battle for independence has not even been fought, and all of us Latin Americans are combatants in this new struggle. The terrible night of battle has *not yet* passed, and the sublime liberty has *not yet* radiated its beams of invincible light. All human beings who remain in chains *have not yet* understood the words of him who died on the cross.[43]

To those who believe that we have emptied the Eucharist of its sacred character, we respond by saying that the history of Latin America, as already suggested, and the content of this history are also the history of salvation, a *locus theologicus,* and a theological word. I must make, however, one other comment. The terms "sacred" and "secular" verbalize or imply a dualistic concept that pits the sacred against the secular. To assert that the Eucharist can be reduced to a mere secular act or to a simple patriotic celebration is once again to be the victim of a dualism alien to Judeo-Christian theology. Moreover, does it make sense to continue talking about patriotic celebrations and religious celebrations? Would it not be better to work out the deeper sense of the former?

I am not attempting here to secularize the sacred, or sacralize the secular. History—the only one we have—is neither sacred nor secular. It has one meaning, and it moves toward one end— namely, the fulfillment of its purpose. Nor do we mean to imply that the secular history of Latin America is related to sacred history in a kind of "intimate" unity and that the Eucharist is a celebration of this "deeper" unity. In a unitary vision of history, the problem consists in relating a *part* (the history of Latin America) with the *whole* (the history of humankind), both of which have the same goal, the Parousia. The Latin American Eucharist celebrates the history of Latin America *and* it celebrates its incorporation into the general history of all humankind. From this it derives its paschal and eschatological meaning, for the paschal mystery of Christ has taken place in it.

It is a Eucharist jealous of its particularity, but "not so as to seal itself off from, but . . . open itself to union with the rest of the world, giving and receiving in a spirit of solidarity."[44]

Apolitical Faith?

The "apolitical" nature of the church is an ideological illusion similar to that of the Prophet Jonah, who dreamed that he was riding a whale when in reality he was wallowing around in its entrails.[45]

To discuss, therefore, whether the eucharistic "moment in which the church is most perfectly itself"[46] is or is not a political act has no meaning. This "moment" has from the beginning been political. The real question is whether the church is exercising its critical political function or is legitimizing the existing political system. Consequently this is not an attempt to suggest a politicizing of the liturgy—given the fact, we repeat, that it has always been politicized. What we are attempting to do is to awaken ourselves to the political character of confirming or reorienting the direction of our political conduct and of making the readjustments necessary in order to do so consciously and effectively.

The Eucharist:

—Is political *in itself* as a result of its own context.

—Is political because it occurs necessarily *in a political context*.

—Is political because, lest it betray its prophetic mission, it has to *confront* its own context with the faith.

—Is political because each of the members who participates *has a line* of political conduct.

—Is political although the political lines of the participants may be *different*.

—Is political although the celebrants are *not aware* of the kind of politics in which they are involved.

—Is political because it *radicalizes* and *energizes* politics.

—Is political because it promotes personalization, socialization, and liberation.

—Is political because it celebrates the utopia *awakened* by creative imagination.

—Is political because it inescapably sows seeds of *nonconformity*.

—Is political because here the real *authenticity* of the faith is measured by political commitment.

—Is political because political commitment demands that the faith *do the truth* (verify) and not merely *preach* the truth (verbalize).

—Is political because it *relativizes* every political scheme no matter how appealing it might appear.

As Besert puts it:

> To the degree that the celebration of the Eucharist is authentic prophecy of a new world, to the degree that all those who celebrate it are sufficiently removed from their habitual situation, to the degree that the Eucharist is celebrated as a true fiesta, the church injects in all its members seeds of protest.
>
> If they believe that they are hopelessly bound to certain servitudes, it is here that they glimpse that this order of things is not inevitable. If they accept with resignation society as it is or as it has been forced upon them, the creative imagination, awakened by the celebration of the utopia, reveals to them that there are other possible schemes and designs for society.
>
> The Eucharist can be an anesthetic or an evasion. But it

can also be the seed of revolution that awakens the mind to what is possible, to what is not yet achieved, to what has not yet even been contemplated by the creative imagination. It is no accident that the celebration of the passover was preceded in Israel many times by political rebellions against foreign occupation.[47]

The eucharistic gesture, as we have said, takes place necessarily in a political context and cannot avoid a confrontation with faith. When St. Ambrose of Milan communicated to Emperor Theodosius that he could not celebrate the Mass in the Emperor's presence because of his brutal slaughter of innocent persons in Thessalonica, when Pope Vigilius brought to the very heart of the liturgical celebration the siege of Rome (A.D. 537), when in Bolivia protest Masses are celebrated because of unjust repressions, when in Colombia the same thing is done in order to raise questions about the social system—all these examples manifest the deep conviction that the *Eucharist must not* take place without relationship to the political context, and that it cannot be celebrated without judging the political context.

One case can be cited that needs little comment. The archbishop of Asunción, Paraguay, Ismael Rolón, refused to celebrate the traditional Te Deum of thanksgiving on the day of national independence "*as a clear and calculated protest against the state of violence to which the Christian community was being subjected.*" Archbishop Rolón explained the reasons for his refusal:

> When the freedom and rights that are linked to the community are systematically violated; when liberation is no more than a word; when the Christian community and its church are openly suffocated in the exercise of their life and evangelical mission of liberation, a liturgical celebration of thanksgiving referring to the heroic deeds of national independence would be meaningless.[48]

The truth is that the refusal to celebrate the Te Deum was a most articulate liturgy, for it expressed very clearly the *prophetic* word directed against the "lords" of Paraguay.

In the "moment in which the church is most perfectly itself," it cannot renounce its prophetic mission. It is not possible to present the body of the Lord in its eucharistic *kerygma* in a den of thieves or in a cave of cowards who want no part of being involved in the problems of the people; that would be to abandon Jesus' commitment to humanity.

We may certainly assume that any liturgical celebration will inevitably take place within a political context, and that this context will not be without a religious significance.[49] The Eucharist is contextualized, not celebrated *in vacuo*, and we should have the courage to recognize it. Better said, the meaning of reality cannot be separated from the vicissitudes of history.

For this reason those who attend the Eucharist have already—or at least should have—their directions of political commitment, though usually they are different and even at times opposed. What should we do in view of this fact? Flee from this intraecclesial conflictual situation? No, quite the contrary. It should be confronted. Those who come together, if they are truly Christians, and if in fact they are convinced of their common destiny, should not only be able to come together but also should be able to debate in turn the political means conducive for reaching their stated goals. They should confront their political theses with their faith and should be disposed to the Christian community's judging the quality of their political action together with the eventual compatibility or lack of compatibility with the politics of the gospel. In this way the Eucharist will become a kind of workshop of faith and a laboratory of history. De Clercq expresses it thus:

> It should also be possible for part of this liturgy to consist of a discussion of political points of view so long as there is a strict adherence to the principle that those representing each side in this political debate make their religious motivations clear and are ready to pray together.[50]

In this way faith would not only question political commitment, but this questioning by the faith would demand authenticity and concrete acts. Both would make their mutual demands and both would achieve something by them. Those unaware of the political stakes would also be awakened from their apolitical sleep and be forced to implement their faith with an effective political praxis. In summary there would be an awakening of the consciousness of one's historical responsibility beyond the intimate relationship between God and me, and the privatized relationship between you and me.

We believe that the politicizing of the liturgy (namely, an awareness of its political character) is not an attempt to popularize the liturgy, nor a simple therapy against boredom among the faithful, and certainly not a calculated design to attract Christians who have withdrawn from the church. It is, we believe, a gesture of responsibility against implicit support of political programs which Christians explicitly do not want to support. Nothing is more dangerous, we repeat, than unrecognized power. One must ask, therefore, is it not possible that the depoliticization of the liturgy is the fundamental reason why the Eucharist has little or no attraction for the majority of males?

The Eucharist as the Cultual Objectification of History

In the first part of this work we saw that one of the peculiarities of Israel consisted in its having produced a new ritualistic form, converting religious rites into a system of objectifying their historical exploits. Is it possible also for the Eucharist to objectify our history (the diachronic aspect) and also our sociological structure (the synchronic)?

One may respond in two ways. Above all we should keep in mind that the church is a structural sign in which the messages in their totality can be different from their parts.[51] The command of Jesus, "Do this"—which refers primarily to his giving of himself for the people, and secondarily to the ritualistic commemoration of this giving—binds the protagonist of the event to the gestures, the words, and the elements that were utilized in the celebration to predict it.

"This," therefore, is the community that celebrates Christ's giving of himself for the people, but also the natural elements that were not in their "native" state but were the "fruit of human labor." This may be diagramed as follows:

Sign: Human Beings (subject)—the ecclesial community

                  Elements (object)—bread and wine, fruit of human
                  labor.

Content: Our own history as the Body of Christ in gestation
                  of the *Total* Christ mediating the dialectic of death
                  (oppression) and resurrection (liberation).

When, therefore, we affirm that the Eucharist is (or should be)
the objectification of our history, *we understand that the objectification is an action* (acted out by the ecclesial community) and
not a thing (bread and wine). These are the elements utilized in an
objectifying action, but they are not the objectification itself.
They derive their significance from the general context of the eucharistic action. The community, therefore, does not objectify the
history in the elements (bread and wine) but in the total eucharistic *act* that comprehends these gestures, words, and elements. The
significance cannot be monopolized by one single component of
objectifying action, and one who "reads" the sign cannot decom-
pose it (chemically) in order to retain only the significance of one
of these elements (bread and wine). It is the total act that has
significance, not the parts.

But someone will ask, "Is it not the church that is objectified in
the eucharistic action? Furthermore, is it not the history of all the
Latin American church that we should be celebrating and not the
history of one particular people?" What is it, therefore, that the
church objectifies in the Eucharist? Its own mystery or that of
humanity?

We must remember that the church does not possess its own
private mystery. What is particular to the church is its awareness
of the mystery—and from this it derives its responsibility.

The forward thrust of the Parousia is not something "owned"
by the church: it belongs to humanity as such; it is humankind's
forward thrust. It follows from this that the church does not have
its own future course. The only future projection that the church
can assume is that of humankind. And if the church joins forces
with humanity in this venture, it is not for the purpose of superim-

posing the church's future on that of humankind. The church can only *participate* in the unique forward thrust of history. Its own future depends on it.[52]

Inasmuch as the Eucharist is that "moment in which the church is most perfectly itself," it cannot be an act of narcissistic self-contemplation contradicting its purpose for being in the world. The Eucharist is fundamentally *an act in which the church measures its centrifugal character*, aware that it is celebrating a venture that is not its own private property but is simply the expression of humanity moving toward its own final destiny.

When humanity, here represented by the church, proclaims, "This is my Body," it is affirming itself—and "the fruit of human labor" (concretized in the bread and the wine)—to be the Body of Christ, the Total Christ. But the church is not only this, for with the eyes of faith and the tools of social analysis we understand that this Body is broken, it is torn and divided between exploiters and exploited.[53] Therefore, if we are asked what it is that we present to the Father as the Body of Christ, the answer is that we present the Body as we have discovered it with socio-analytical tools as the broken and divided Body. The "bread of offertory" actually presents to humanity a Body that is torn and broken, the same Body that is presented to the Father. "This is my Body" becomes "This is my Body divided among exploiters and exploited." Those who see Christ in this way cannot avoid sensing the challenge to break down the ignominious "wall of separation" in order to create from the two a single new humanity (Eph. 2:15).

That Christ is *also* in the bread and in the wine implies that he is not only human, but also "the fruit of human labor," by which human beings humanize nature and also humanize themselves. This implies further that the process of elaboration of this fruit-of-labor is not alien to the process of christogenesis, and that in it Christ places (offers, proposes) himself before us as the fruit of our "gestation," *obligating us to evaluate our offering and the human process that precedes and defines the offering—that is, the social relationships of production hidden under the appearances of bread and wine*. The real is not only the material (a piece of bread), but also what is produced. The source of the bread (as a cultural product) is human labor.[54]

It remains therefore that the bread and the wine are not objectified in the Eucharist as part of a material, reified cosmos, but as a product of a properly social phenomenon of sharing a meal, of taking together. Nor are the bread and wine to be "swallowed as is"; they are to be examined and judged (critically, as in a *krisis*) before being eaten, with a view to righting the social relationships of production that precede and shape the fruit of human labor. Communicants, emulating their teacher Jesus Christ, will focus their attention not only on the thing presented (offered, proposed), but also on the human action that precedes and defines it.[55]

The bread and the wine are not there simply as themselves, nor simply as something material, much less as something magical. They are there as products of the community that celebrates its labor, its results, and its manner of production.

The question is not so analogical as it may appear, for it deals with a "collective organism" (the Total Christ) that should re-evaluate continually the way it produces the fruit of its labor (bread and wine, although not necessarily these things alone) in order to establish whether it is diverting or blocking the auto-gestation of the Parousia of humankind. It is a question of onto-genesis, of anthropogenesis, of christogenesis.

For this reason when the fruit of human labor is being exploited by a minority, the Parousia—the full possession and enjoyment of this fruit—is blocked by those who are depriving the community of its increase in value. In order to prevent this anomaly, the church celebrating the Eucharist should despoil the exploiters in order to recover the fruit of labor (the Body of Christ) for the whole community. In this way the Body of Christ will not be appropriated by a few.

Objectification of Our Structural Center

We have already said that the experience of the exodus was "the central event around which the Hebrews organized their total per-ception of reality" (Harvey Cox). On the other hand, we have seen that they objectified this principle of organization and in-terpretation of reality, and that in doing so they favored (or deter-mined) the characterization of themselves as a people and of the permanent source of the nourishment of their faith. Here they learned and reviewed the history of their community and the liberating acts of Yahweh.

What is the "structuring center" around which we should organize our basic perception of reality? It would appear to be *our first independence*, because it is in reference to it that we discover our "personality" as offspring of the "prepotent Hispanic father" and of the indigenous violated mother.[56] It is here in the confluence of these two genetic and cultural sources (one European and the other of Asiatic origin) that we begin to recognize our past and also our historical identity, even though with many lacunae. The first rebellion was the self-affirmation of our personality and existence (I rebel, therefore I exist, as Albert Camus would say).

Our historical memory goes back to the traumatic fact that an aggressive and voracious "father" violated (he did not seduce) an unsuspecting and naive "servant." Herein began our history as children of a slave and not as free persons; we were dependent from the beginning. This is the reason why the feats of our first independence—as imperfect as they might have been—are an indication of our emancipative possibilities, a reminder of the self-affirmation of our own "personality" confronting colonizers, and a harbinger of our complete liberation. For this reason we need to objectify our first liberation in the paschal celebration not only to connect it to its own plenitude, but also to nourish our faith, review our own emancipative attempts, and finally define ourselves as a people. Only in this way can the consciousness of our historical destiny be awakened.

How can we recognize ourselves in a Eucharist in which "the structuring center" of our own corporate "personality" is not the center of our celebration? Would a liturgy be authentically Latin American in which the characteristic features of our own "countenance" were only peripheral and secondary?

How, therefore, can we incorporate into the Eucharist this "structuring center" without displacing the other center who is Christ? Someone will ask, "Is Christ the center of the Eucharist, or are the events of independence the center?" "Will it be christocentric, or anthropocentric, or temporal?"

It would appear, in the first place, that Christians without knowing it transfer to their christology the circular and spherical

scheme of the Hegelian concept of society and of history. For
Hegel a historical formalization densifies into a determined form
or essence, unifying and totalizing it, and refracting it into all its
categories or spheres. Each historical epoch was characterized by
a determined formalization. (Rome, for example, was "formed"
by its exaltation of law.) This form was the "circle of circles," the
"sphere of spheres." It radiated into all the others; it was ubiqui-
tous and all-pervasive.[57]

When this conceptualization is transferred to the church, it is
verbalized in such expressions as christocentric, christocentricity,
Christ the center, Christ the keystone, around whom all things
"revolve." In this, as in all topical metaphors, a theological datum
is represented by a geometrical figure—the circle, the sphere. We
do not reject the need our knowledge has of these topical images,
which moreover are not exclusive to theology. Marx, for example,
also spoke of infra- and super-structures, thus utilizing an archi-
tectural image of human society.

What we want to emphasize is that this circular scheme emascu-
lates christology, making us human beings the irrelevant periph-
ery, irrelevant to the Total Christ. It is as if we were the christologi-
cal surplus. At the hermeneutical level this signifies that only the
biblical word (Christ included) is the center and that all others are
in the world of shadows, incapable of speaking their word. Such a
theology can only be applied, adapted, or accommodated to the
Latin American reality but in no way reinterpreted by the word
that God speaks to us from within our continent.

A Christ without his "members" is not the Total Christ.
Without a body there is no head, and without the head the body is
decapitated. St. Augustine, faithfully interpreting St. Paul, said
that we are the Total Christ: "There are many human beings and
they are one thing; there are many Christians and they are one
Christ. Christians with their head who ascended into heaven are
the one Christ: not that he is one and we are many, but that we
many are one in him. There is therefore one man—Christ, head
and body." [58]

If a geometric image is necessary, we propose an elliptic Christology, an elliptic evangelization, an elliptic hermeneutic, and an
elliptic Eucharist. In all of these the outstanding feature would be
the *dialectical* articulation of the two "centers": Christ and the

Latin American in the first place, the situation of Christ and our situation in the second place, the biblical word and the word from Latin America in the third place, the paschal deed and our own liberating deeds in the fourth place. The circle, having a single center, does not appear therefore to be adequate to "geometrize" the dialectical bipolarity of these two variants. The ellipse, on the other hand, with its two "centers," ably does so.

The Eucharist so understood would establish for us a more adequate relationship with Christian tradition because it would be the *kerygmatic* proclamation of the paschal deed of Jesus Christ, the radical liberation of the entire person and of all persons, the basic act that suggests the possibility and the meaning of our own liberation. Remember that "the Risen Christ . . . is the goal that the designs of God set for the development of humankind, so that 'we may all reach the stature of the integral person .' "[59] This would guarantee us *continuity*.

On the other hand, to celebrate our historical deeds and to become aware of the social relationsips of production hidden in the appearances of bread and wine, we would reevaluate our incipient independence as the "anticipation of complete redemption in Christ," and it would implant in us the conviction that "all 'growth in humanity' brings us closer to 'reproducing the image of the Son so that he will be the firstborn among many brothers and sisters.' "[60] In contrast, it would force us to revise the christo-genetic process that precedes and defines "the fruit of human labor." In this there would be a fundamental *discontinuity*.

The Affirming Context of the Eucharist

We earlier emphasized (Chap. 1) that in Old Testament times there were religious festivals that tended to readjust social inequalities. This was possible within the socio-cultural framework of Israel because their laws and organization were at one and the same time religious and juridico-political. Today, however, the church does not have the power to declare laws as was done in ancient time when debts were pardoned, slaves were liberated, and deprived owners reclaimed their properties. Moreover, even if the church could do this today, it is doubtful whether there would be a periodic attempt to enact laws that would readjust social inequalities. The problem consists rather in struggling for the creation of *objective conditions* that will make fellowship, justice, and peace possible.

We believe that at this historical moment *the only legitimate context for the Eucharist—a Eucharist such as we have proposed—is one in solidarity with the movement for the liberation of our continent*, and more concretely with the exploited classes of our society. Any declared alliance with the dominant classes will create an emasculated context for the Eucharist, given the fact that such a tactic eliminates with the "right hand" all that the "left hand" accomplishes.

A community celebration of the Eucharist solemnly commits all Christians to struggle actively against everything that discriminates against and disintegrates humanity. It is a sacrilege, according to St. Paul, when a Christian community, after having received the same bread and the same wine, continues to maintain social, economic, and cultural differences under the pretext that a mystical unity has been established. If church assemblies are, to the observers of the contemporary world, signs of separation that emphasize class differences and the retention of privileges, at that moment the church automatically ceases to be the church because it is not a productive sign of the unity of the human genus.[61]

It cannot be otherwise if the total language of the institutional church is contradicted by the eucharistic word we proclaim. Even though we shout loudly and clearly something different, there would still exist a contradictory gap. Instead of this anomaly, the Eucharist should be the socio-political reactivator and the occasion of confrontation in which the church judges its commitment to the interests of the socially exploited class. The church's option therefore must be clear and sharp. Any accommodation will reduce its role to that of being a lubricant of the social system, and "this mode of approaching the problem moves easily to an ideology of unity without conflict"[62] and ignores and disparages the real conditions of the paschal dynamic in which only a church that dares to "drink his cup" can expect Christ's resurrection.

To opt for the poor does not mean only a vocation of poverty. It implies also supporting the cause of the poor, identifying openly with them against those who oppress and burden them. For this reason the class struggle should not be left aside, for the goal is not the *"reduction of tensions" but the overcoming of them*, creating better conditions of life for those who—until now—have lived with rejection, ignominy, and oppression. To manifest solidarity with the poor in the class struggle presupposes a radical reorientation of the community of faith. It will no longer be the pillar of the established order (as during the time when the church supported the Constantinian government), but an element that challenges the established order. From being an instrument of preservation the church will become an agent of transformation, and rather than defending decrepit orders of creation (which in itself, because of the transformations it undergoes, is always decrepit and renewing itself at the same time) the church will try to implement the order of the announced new creation. Here the disadvantaged will be the privileged, and the last will be first.[63]

When Christians celebrate the Eucharist and are really committed to the interests and struggles of the oppressed, this solidarity (conviction and option) cannot but affect the general structure of eucharistic action. In the first place it will affect eucharistic action by means of a deserved respect for its forms of expression, its festivities, and its rites, and in the second place by the relationship (incarnation) of the Eucharist with its cultural world. The Old Testament prophets, rather than attacking the agricultural celebrations of the Canaanites, connected these rites to the exodus and gave them a historical meaning that removed them from idolatry. The prophets of today will know how to relate the agricultural festivities of our *campesinos* and the rites of our workers with the paschal deed of the Eucharist in which, as we have already said, there will also be included our emancipative deeds. What the *campesinos* and agricultural workers need to understand—inclined by the nature of their work to begin again what is already begun—is that they have a history, a past, a relation with the whole social system of production, and that they have a destiny. There is no other occasion more propitious for awakening our people to structural contradictions than when they celebrate the "maternity" of nature, which, made fertile by human effort, gives birth to the fruit of labor, labor that can be laid bare in eucharistic action in order to discern its christogenetic inner nature.

To contextualize these festivities in the general framework of a

history that moves toward its fulfillment is to relativize and tem-
poralize them. But we can thus eliminate the idolatrous dangers
inherent in cosmological rites and also free them from the recid-
ivistic scheme of the eternal return, which from the sociological
point of view is the sacralization of intra-systemic fatalism. Or to
put it another way, it is the absolutization of the impossibility of
an act that would be really trans-systemic.[64]

Koinonia of the Word, of the Bread, and of Possessions

Of the Word. How many times have we heard Christians com-
plain of the loneliness that they experience when participating in
the Eucharist. "We go every Sunday," they say, "and we see faces,
but we don't know who they are." Those present do not know
each other either in the Greek or in the biblical sense. How can
they reach out to each other, communicate, share their problems,
their anxieties, their doubts, their questions, if there is no opportunity to share the word? It is not only the biblical word that
should be spoken in the assembly; it is also the everyday word, the
word of our common experience, in order that from sharing there
will emerge the demands of *the Word.* Only by establishing these
kinds of conditions can the everyday word be shared and thus will
it be possible to practice the communion of communication. This
would break down many walls of isolation and permit persons to
reveal themselves and speak *their* word.

Why all this verticalism of the word? Because we have made the
celebration of our sacrament or passover so sophisticated that we
have "packaged" it, we have filled it with formalism to such a
degree that no one dares to speak. Silence is more a symbol of fear
than an indication of praise. No one dares to speak because they
fear being "out of place," and it would appear that the average
believer therefore has neither voice nor vote and that our daily
experiences are really of no importance. Faith and daily life are
permanently severed.

*Why not welcome in the Eucharist the voice of those without
voice*, the prophetic voice, the contesting voice, the voice of the
poor who have no access to any other means of communication?
Is it not the responsibility of the church to make the voice of the
silenced and suppressed resonant in the eucharistic environment?

Don't we say that the poor are the visible face of Christ in the world? And that the oppressed masses are suffering even now his passion? And that through them Christ is now speaking his word? And if we do not hear them, are we not turning our backs on Christ? And if we refuse to hear them, are we not refusing to hear him?

Of the Bread. Sharing the word will prepare for the communion of the bread, of the wine, and of the food. All those participating in the celebration should bring their contribution to the Lord's supper, for only in this way can they share the bread. In reality, we repeat, those who do not practice the *koinonia* of food (of the bread) do not discern that *though many, we are one Body, because we share the one bread,* and they do not discern the ecclesial Body of Christ.

In other words they do not see the church in the multitude of Christians who gather for the sacrament. Even less do they see Christ in the plurality of his members. They do not see the church or Christ as the sources of universal communion. Nor do they feel challenged by the economic, political, and cultural differences. If the bread, as we have said, is the fruit of labor, to share the bread is to share the results of our labor, and it can be the grounds for discovering our labor as collaboration.

No one, therefore, who is monopolizing the fruit of labor can celebrate the Eucharist with a clear conscience. How could Christ consecrate the fruit of despoliation? Who could share the fruits of work without discovering that this bread is the result of co-labor and co-elaboration? Who can share the fruit of labor who has not participated in its production? Even more, can the church share the fruit of labor in a society divided between exploiters and exploited? Can the church consecrate the fruit of labor (bread and wine) without "consecrating" the social relationships of production that make work possible? Or is this bread come down from heaven not incarnated in the bread that is offered up from the earth?

Of Possessions. What is said here is implicit in what has been said above. The Eucharist should promote the creation of human communities with an original form of economico-communitarian infrastructure that will shore up communion-union in the faith. At the same time, and to the degree possible within the system, it should demonstrate the practicability of utopia by heralding a universal communion to which one cannot come without committing oneself to the creation of the objective infrastructural conditions necessary. The sharing of possessions should have no other meaning.

Great doses of hidden manichaeism anesthetize the conscience of many Christians who prefer "mystical" or merely religious community to human community.

A Eucharist in which this genuine threefold *koinonia* is practiced will be an authentic protest against the monologue of individualism, against the monopolization of the fruit of human labor, and against the atomization and division of humankind between exploiters and exploited. This would be a true cultural revolution.

Conclusion

To conclude we want to point out that the interests of contemporary humanity move progressively and increasingly toward the political. To attempt an ostensibly apolitical liturgy in a world essentially political is absurd—unless one wants to banish the Eucharist from history. In this case a policy of withdrawal from the world has been adopted. And if withdrawal is effected consciously, we can only suspect that it is being done to separate the people from their concern with this world.

On the other hand, it appears that today it is impossible for the church to be composed of members whose political interests are antagonistic (not merely different), and with good reason, because the Eucharist cannot be celebrated by persons who are radically divergent in regard to their political designs. Participation in the same Mass by persons of opposing social classes has been possible only by the anonymity that frequently characterizes the composition of the church.[65] A hypothesis that consciously attempts to reconcile antagonistic classes means that there has been acceptance of a Eucharist put at the service of a divided society. It consequently opposes the movement for the elimination of classes. It is therefore a Eucharist consciously at the service of the status quo.

For a conciliationist ecclesiology *the subjects of a eucharistic celebration* can be the members of all social classes. But for an ecclesiology that sees itself affected by the division of classes, the subjects of the eucharistic celebration can be only the members of the socially exploited class and their effective allies, including converts coming from the exploiting class.

We confirm therefore from another point of view what we stated earlier, that the only legitimate context for the Eucharist is one of ecclesial solidarity with the undertaking of the liberation of the oppressed, because the poor and the oppressed cannot be isolated abstractly from the social class to which they belong. This implies solidarity with the exploited class and conflict with the exploiting class. Therefore the only persons qualified to participate in this celebration are those working for liberation, with the understanding that this implies the suppression of the objective conditions that make it possible for some to be exploited and others to be exploiters.

Unity is the final goal and not the point of departure, and to reach it, it is necessary to embrace the essential conflict in order to destroy the real causes of division. To assume that the church can be a "place of worship for all" is to confuse the church with the kingdom of God and paralyze the movement of history toward the kingdom. The Eucharist retains therefore the same ambiguity and conflict inherent in history, and only those who truly accompany Christ in his work of the paschalization of society can truly participate. Excluding one or more social sectors is not done with the malicious intention of excluding them from the kingdom, but precisely the opposite, in the hope that they can eventually become a part of the kingdom.

In this way the Eucharist is not reduced to a mere positivist reflection of the class society, but rather becomes the prophetic judgment not only on the celebration itself, but also on the restriction of participation. That only one social segment can celebrate the Eucharist is a prophetic and challenging judgment.

We conclude by stating explicitly that the Eucharist and the liturgy in general appear to be *a kind of symbolico-structural exegesis of history.* As interpretation, it should utilize socio-analytic instruments, and it cannot avoid the ambiguity of all interpretation. As symbolic, it should utilize the same symbols that the people utilize to celebrate their history. As exegesis *of history,* the content of that exegesis should be history. The Eucharist will be in this way a hermeneutical variant of history, celebrative and evaluative of the historical process. It will be a hermeneutic that is in a certain sense imitative, in a certain sense dramatic, but always in constitutive reference to the historical event.

Notes

Introduction

1. All biblical quotations are from the Jerusalem Bible (1968), unless otherwise noted.

2. Ludovico Silva, *Teoría y práctica de la ideología* (Mexico: Nuestro Tiempo, 1971), p. 215. Cited by Hugo Assmann, *Teología desde la praxis de la liberación* (Salamanca: Sígueme, 1973), p. 258.

3. See my article, "Profecía, interpretación y reinterpretación," *Teología, evangelización y liberación* (Bogotá: Paulinas, 1973), pp. 61–70, and "La profecía en América Latina," an unpublished lecture given in 1973 in the Seminario de Teología Latinoamericana.

Chapter One

1. John Bright, *A History of Israel* (Philadelphia: Westminster, 1972), p. 91.

2. Ur was in southern Mesopotamia; Haran lay to the northwest of Mesopotamia. Italics added.

3. For a more detailed discussion, see Roland de Vaux, *Ancient Israel: Its Life and Institutions*, trans. John McHugh (New York: McGraw-Hill, 1961), pp. 278–288.

4. Ibid., p. 289.

5. S. Pongutá, "El culto," *Encuentro* 73 (Nos. 33–34):6.

6. Georges Auzou, *De la servidumbre al servicio* (Madrid, Fax), p. 182. From the French edition *De la servitude au service; étude du livre de l'Exode* (Paris: Editions de l'Orante, 1961).

7. Ibid., p. 184.

8. Rafael Avila, *La liberación* (Bogotá: Voluntad, 1971), pp. 37–38.

9. Harvey Cox, *The Secular City* (New York: Macmillan, 1965), p. 26.

10. According to José Porfirio Miranda, "Today we can assert with certainty (although it might give scandal) that the covenant was *not* the form in which the law was originally connected with Yahweh." The concept of the covenant is from the seventh century and for this reason the

Sinaitic account (Exodus 19 and Numbers 10) is a much later insertion. Miranda continues: "If we keep in mind that the Sinaitic account (Exod. 19 and Num. 10) is a much later narrative insertion, then the conclusion is unequivocal: Israel's adoption of laws was originally connected with the libertarian (exodus) tradition and the laws were adopted 'in order to do justice between a man and his neighbor.' " *Marx and the Bible*, trans. John Eagleson (Maryknoll, N.Y.: Orbis, 1974), pp. 140, 144-145.

During discussions in the seminary where I first had the privilege of testing the content of this work, there emerged a tendency to resist any admission of the primacy and fundamental character of the exodus. Furthermore, because of the lack of evidence whereby the primacy of the exodus could be negated, many students were content to give equal status to the covenant. The usual approach was to affirm that the exodus and the covenant were the two tracks on which the community of Israel had moved forward. It is impossible to support this thesis, in my judgment, if the biblical data are respected. The exodus is basic and the covenant is on a second level. It is a derivative event, not a primary one. This is not to say that the covenant lacks importance, but rather to insist that its impact is relative and secondary.

11. De Vaux, *Ancient Israel*, pp. 258, 259.

12. Cox, *The Secular City,* p. 55.

13. Ibid.

14. Ibid., p. 56.

15. See note in the Jerusalem Bible on Lev. 25:14.

16. De Vaux, *Ancient Israel,* p. 491.

17. Ibid., p. 490.

18. Ibid., p. 333.

19. Claude Tresmontant, *La doctrina moral de los profetas de Israel* (Madrid: Taurus, 1968), p. 108.

20. Ibid., p. 109.

Chapter Two

1. One should keep in mind that these socio-religious movements were not merely religious sects nor simply political parties. They were both religious sects and political parties, and as such they constituted intrinsic elements in the theocratic system—a system in which no distinction was made between state and church, and in which the law was not merely civil or religious but juridico-religious.

2. The Gospel of John places this event at the beginning of Jesus' public ministry and adds details not included in the synoptic accounts, e.g., "Making a whip out of some cord, he drove them all out of the temple, cattle and sheep as well, scattered the money changers' coins,

knocked their tables over and said to the pigeon sellers, 'Take all of this out of here and stop turning my Father's house into a market' " (2:15-16).

3. Primitive Christians understood this clearly and refused to receive offerings from those *"qui pauperes opprimunt"* (who oppress the poor), as St. Basil declared when he refused the offering of an unjust prefect. See *Diálogo Social*, No. 46, pp. 21–22.

4. It appears certain that according to John 18:23 and other texts describing the passion the paschal supper was celebrated that year on the evening of Friday (*parasceve* in Matthew 27:62 and John 19:14, 31, 42, probably means the Jewish day of passover preparation). It is translated in the Jerusalem Bible as the Jewish Day of Preparation; the New English Bible (1970) has "the eve of Passover." The Lord's supper, which the synoptic writers place the day before, i.e., on Thursday evening, can thus be seen as anticipatory of the Jewish rite—or more likely as the anticipation of Jesus himself. He would be unable to celebrate the passover the following day except in his own body on the cross. See the note on Matthew 26:17 in the Jerusalem Bible.

5. Max Thurian refers to the text that very probably was utilized in the time of Jesus and notes confidently that this blessing of the bread and wine or thanksgiving had nothing to do with the consecration of the elements in any magical sense: *The Eucharistic Memorial*, trans. J. G. Davis, 2 vols. (London: Lutterworth, 1961, and Richmond, Va.: John Knox Press, 1961), 2:43–45.

6. Ibid., 1:28.

7. Ibid.

8. Ibid., 1:16.

9. Ibid., 1:21.

10. Ibid., 1:22

11. Bernard Besert, *Tomorrow a New Church*, trans. Matthew J. O'Connell (New York: Paulist Press, 1973), p. 114.

12. Those, such as Max Thurian, who explain this gesture by Israel's liturgical traditions alone limit the sign to the liturgical context and ignore the fact that this context was permeated with the historico-political implications of the event in process—which, in the last analysis, inspired the gesture of Jesus. The background is the total event itself, not the religious rite.

13. Miranda, *Marx and the Bible*, p. 192.

14. A. Robert and A. Feuillet, eds., *Introduction to the Old Testament* (New York: Desclée, 1968), pp. 264–265. This two-volume work of the Old and the New Testaments originally appeared in French, *Introduction à la Bible* (Tournai, Belgium: Desclée and Cie, 1959).

15. The temple was destroyed by the Roman legions of Titus in August

A.D. 70. If 1 Corinthians was written in approximately 57, and 1 Peter in 64, then the hypothesis that Paul was referring to the destruction of the temple appears unlikely. One should note, however, that the dates ascribed to the writing of these epistles are less than certain.

16. Yves Congar has developed this concept extensively in his work *The Mystery of the Temple*, trans. Reginald F. Trevett (Westminster, Md.: Newman, 1962).

17. Max Meinertz, *Teología del Nuevo Testamento* (Madrid: Fax, 1966), p. 256.

18. A. Robert and A. Feuillet, eds., *Introduction to the New Testament* (New York: Desclée, 1965), p. 410.

19. A. Rincón, *La Hora*, No. 68.

20. See the works of Jean-Marie Tillard, *L'Eucaristie, pâque de l'Eglise* (Paris: Cerf, 1964), and Oscar Cullmann, *La foi et le culte de l'Eglise primitive* (Neuchâtel: Delachaux & Niestlé, 1963), especially Parts 4 and 5 on "Le culte dans l'Eglise primitive" and "Les sacrements dans l'Evangile Johanique."

21. The words *koinonia estin tou aimatos* and *koinonia tou somatos* do not appear to be correctly translated "communion with." They should be rendered "communion *of* " and include the "owning of everything in common"—that is, *koinonia* of bread-body and wine-blood. These expressions make the declaration more understandable: "The fact that there is only one loaf means that though there are many of us, we form a single body because we all have a share in this one loaf" (1 Cor. 10:17).

22. See José Castillo, "La Eucaristía, problema político," *Diálogo Social*, No. 46, p. 20.

23. Didache 14:2; *The Apostolic Fathers: a Translation and Commentary*, Vol. 3, "Barnabas and the Didache," by Robert A. Kraft (New York: Nelson, 1965), p. 173.

24. Didache 9:4; ibid., p. 166.

25. *The First Apology of Justin Martyr*, I, 67, 6.

26. Cyprian, *Treatise*, VIII, "On Works and Almsgiving," 15.

27. *Constitutions of the Holy Apostles*, II, Sec. 17, 1–5. Cf. II, Sec. 4, 25.

28. ". . . qui pauperes opprimunt" according to the *Statuta Ecclesiae Antiqua*, 69. Cf. *Constitutions of the Holy Apostles*, II, Sec. 8; IV, Sec. 2, 6–8.

29. Ibid., IV, Sec. 2, 6.

30. *Didascalia Apostolorum*, IV, 8, 1–2.

31. Ambrose, Letter LI, 13.

32. *The Panegyric on Saint Basil*, XLIII, 50–52; Cf. Gregory Nazianzen, Oratio 43:52.

33. Irenaeus, *Against Heresies*, IV, 18, 2.

34. See "Hacia una liturgia encarnada," a report done by the students of IPLA in Bogotá, Colombia, 1973, pp. 9–10 (manuscript).

35. Ibid., pp. 12–13.

36. Ibid., p. 9.

37. Paris de Grassi was known for his dry wit, especially regarding ecclesiastical ceremonies. On one occasion, for example, he said of Leo X: "He left Rome without a stole, and what is worse, without his rochet, and worst of all, with boots on. That is quite improper, for no one can kiss his feet." R. L. Foley, "Grassi," *New Catholic Encyclopedia* VI: 705 (Tr.)

38. "Hacia una liturgia encarnada," pp. 15–17.

39. Max Thurian, *The Eucharistic Memorial* (1960), 1:9.

40. Cited in ibid., pp. 12–13.

41. See Edward Schillebeeckx, *La presencia de Cristo en la Eucaristía* (Madrid: Fax, 1968); in Eng. see *Eucharist* (New York: Sheed and Ward, 1968) and *Christ: The Sacrament of the Encounter with God* (New York: Sheed and Ward, 1963).

42. Thurian, *The Eucharistic Memorial,* 1:51–53.

43. See Claude Tresmontant, *A Study of Hebrew Thought*, trans. Michael F. Gibson (New York: Desclée, 1960), pp. 90–91.

44. "Constitution on the Sacred Liturgy," 36:1, 2. *The Teachings of Vatican Council II* (Westminster, Md.: Newman, 1966).

45. See note 37 above.

46. Constitution on the Sacred Liturgy, 59. Italics added.

47. Ibid., 119.

48. Ibid., 116, 120.

49. Ibid., 123.

50. Ibid., 1.

51. Ibid., 21. Italics added.

52. Ibid., 37.

53. Ibid., 43.

54. Miranda, *Marx and the Bible*, p. 284.

Chapter Three

1. See C. J. McNaspy, "Liturgy," *The Documents of Vatican II* (New York: Guild Press, 1966), p. 133.

2. Constitution on the Sacred Liturgy, 10.

3. Medellín, "Liturgy," 4; English translation, CELAM, *The Church in the Present-Day Transformation of Latin America in the Light of the Council,* Vol. II Conclusions, (Washington, D.C.: Latin American Bureau, USCC, 1968); hereafter referred to as Medellín.

4. Ibid.

5. Avila uses here the phrase, "meta volante," well understood by Latin Americans in reference to bicycle racing. It designates an intermediate point such as the goal of a day's race, but not the final goal, because a race continues for several days. The *meta volante* is usually the highest point of a long ascent and special prizes are given to the racers who reach it first (Tr.).

6. Medellín, "Catechesis," 4.

7. Ibid., Introduction to the Final Documents; "Presence of the Church in the Present-Day Transformation of Latin America," 5.

8. Ibid.

9. Paul VI, *Populorum progressio,* 20; cf. Avila, *Elementos para una evangelización liberadora* (Salamanca; Sígueme, 1971), p. 138.

10. Constitution on the Sacred Liturgy, 59; italics to indicate the pedagogical finality of sacramental signs.

11. Ibid., 109b.

12. Medellín, "Liturgy," 2.

13. See *Denuncia,* No. 41, p. 6.

14. Medellín, "Liturgy," 6e.

15. Roger Garaudy, "Il inaugure un noveau mode d'existence," *Lumière et Vie* 112 (April-May, 1973), p. 16.

16. There are many studies now on this particular theme; e.g., Gilberto Giménez, "La dimensión socio-política de la práctica de la fe," *Contacto* 1 (February 1973); the whole of *Servir,* no. 44; and Concilium 84, *Political Commitment and Christian Community.*

17. Medellín, "Peace," 4a.

18. Ibid., 1.

19. Ibid., "Poverty of the Church," 4a.

20. Ibid.

21. See the selection of texts made by MUNIPROC in *Golconda, el libro rojo de los Curas rebeldes* (Bogotá, 1969), p. 94.

22. See Segundo Galilea, "Bases históricas para una renovación de los ministerios, *¿A los pobres se les anuncia el Evangelio?* Col. IPLA, No. 11 (Bogotá: IPLA, 1972), p. 70.

23. In the same letter to Archbishop Isaza, 1965. Cited in *Golconda,* p. 93.

24. Ibid., p. 88.

25. Ibid., p. 87. Italics added.

26. This section relies heavily on Rafael Avila, *La liberación* (Bogotá: Voluntad, 1970), and Segundo Galilea, *¿A los pobres se les anuncia el Evangelio?* (Bogotá: IPLA, 1972).

27. Hugo Assmann, "Implicaciones socioanalíticas e ideológicas del lenguaje de liberación," *Pueblo oprimido, Señor de la Historia* (Montevideo: Tierra Nueva, 1972), p. 166.

28. Avila, *La liberación,* p. 140.

29. Ibid., p. 144.

30. Ibid., pp. 144–146. Italics added.

31. Ibid., p. 148. Italics added.

32. Galilea, *¿A los pobres se les anuncia el Evangelio?* pp. 55–58. Italics added.

33. Ibid., p. 58.

34. See Rafael Avila, *Teología, evangelización y liberación* (Bogotá: Paulinas, 1973), pp. 74ff.

35. Cited by Besert, *Tomorrow a New Church,* p. 92.

36. See *Catequesis Latinoamericana,* No. 16, p. 345.

37. Medellín, "Liturgy," 3. Introduction to the Final Document, 5.

38. Ibid.

39. Avila, *Elementos para una evangelización liberadora,* p. 138.

40. VII Semana Internacional de Catequesis, Comisión 4, No. 3.

41. Paul VI, *Populorum progressio,* 20.

42. Medellín, "Education," 4, 9.

43. Avila, *La Liberación,* p. 177.

44. Medellín (Message to the People of Latin America), p. 42 in English edition.

45. G. Giménez, "La dimensión socio-política de la práctica de la fe," *Contacto* 1 (1973): 37.

46. Medellín, "Liturgy," 3.

47. Besert, *Tomorrow a New Church,* pp. 148–149.

48. Cited in *Revista de Equipos Docentes para América Latina* 24 (December 1973): 23. Italics added.

49. Bertrand de Clercq, "Political Commitment and Liturgical Celebration," Concilium 84, *Political Commitment and Christian Community,* p. 113.

50. Ibid., p. 116.

51. The concept of structure is not easily expressed, but we can attempt a tentative definition. Structure is "a system that presents laws and properties of a totality. These laws of totality are therefore different from the laws or properties of the parts of the system." See Jean Piaget, "Génesis y estructura, en la sicología de la inteligencia," *Seis estudios de sicología* (Barcelona: Seix Barral, 1971), p. 205.

52. See Avila, "La profecía en América Latina," Seminario de Teología Latinoamericana, Bogotá, September, 1973, manuscript.

53. Works dealing specifically with the relation between social classes and Christianity are Giulio Girardi, "Cristianismo y lucha de clases," a lecture given at the University of Deusto, 1969; Noel Olaya, *Unidad cristiana y lucha de clases* (Montevideo: Tierra Nueva, 1972), pp. 57–67; Gustavo Gutiérrez, *A Theology of Liberation* (Maryknoll, N.Y.: Orbis,

1973), pp. 340–349; and Benoit Dumas, *Los dos rostros alienados de la Iglesia una* (Buenos Aires: Latinoamérica Libros, 1971).

54. Enrique Dussel says essentially the same thing in a different context: *Historia de la fe cristiana y cambio social en América Latina* (Salamanca: Sígueme, 1973), p. 75. He cites Marx: "The principal error of all materialisms until now (including that of Feuerbach) consists in making the object the reality; the objective being of sensibility has been understood only under the form of an object, or of an intuition, but not as a tangible human fact, as praxis."

55. See above, Chapter 2, "Camilo Torres and Priorities."

56. The mythical image is that of Enrique Dussel. He writes: "Bartolomé [de las Casas] said of the Indian, referring to the alienation of the indigenous woman, that the mother of Latin America cohabitated with the prepotent Hispanic father, who in turn killed the woman's husband— the Indian—and had children (the *mestizo,* the Latin American) who became the servants." See Dussel's work cited in note 54, pp. 67, 85.

57. Eugenio Trías, *Teoría de las ideologías* (Barcelona: Península, 1970), p. 53.

58. St. Augustine, *Enarratio in Ps. CXXVII,* No. 3, P.L. 37, 1678.

59. Medellín, "Education," 9.

60. Ibid.

61. J. M. González Ruiz, in *Víspera* 6 (1970): 28.

62. Hugo Assmann, *Opresión-Liberación, desafío a los cristianos* (Montevideo: Tierra Nueva, 1971), p. 166.

63. Julio de Santa Ana, "Notas para una ética de liberación a partir de la Biblia," *Pueblo Oprimido, Señor de la Historia* (Montevideo: 1972), pp. 129–130.

64. The masses express this fatalism in statements such as: "Nothing can be done"; "It's the same old story" or "the same old thing"; "All is lost. . . ." It is even more difficult today to convince the people that something can be done when repressive powers are seen as the very embodiment of the apocalyptic beasts.

65. Jean Guichard, *Iglesia, lucha de clases y estrategias políticas* (Salamanca: Sígueme, 1973), p. 45.

Index of Scriptural References

OLD TESTAMENT

General Index